T0368311

A Walk

Down

Memory Lane

Agnes M. (Graf) Weicker

Order this book online at www.trafford.com
or email orders@trafford.com

Most Trafford titles are also available at major online book retailers.

Print information available on the last page.

ISBN: 978-1-4120-2154-8 (sc)
ISBN: 978-1-4122-2122-1 (e)

Trafford rev. 06/23/2018

 www.trafford.com

North America & international
toll-free: 1 888 232 4444 (USA & Canada)
fax: 812 355 4082

PROLOGUE

My family & friends have suggested that while I still have "all my marbles" I should write my memoirs. With all the technology of this millennium– computer, scanner, digital camera and photo-printer at my fingertips, and my "marbles" (I think!) here goes!!

It has been written that "life is like a tapestry - filled with the subtle shadings and brilliant moments which merge together to form the fabric of our experience".

As I sit here on April 5, 2003 and gather my thoughts I realize that my story will be a very personal one about me, my family and my special friends that have made me what I am and have been with me along the path of my seventy-eight (almost seventy-nine) years of life. After all, are we human beings but a product of our heredity and environment? At least that was what we were taught in our first psychology lessons.

I love people. My precious family and friends are the most important beings in my whole life. To me they are the very foundation of my life – as solid as the very ground upon which I walk. The most important ingredient of my life has been love. I was raised as the much loved youngest child in a loving family. I have had the blessing of raising two sons who have shown me much love. As my story unfolds you will hear about the other loves and lovers of my life's journey.

Literary expertise I do not have, but I have never been at a loss for words, so with memory and imagination I will put some of those thoughts on paper. This novel was originally meant for family only as it reveals some of my most private thoughts and memories. I will enclose some pictures that will accompany the accounts to make everything more readable and believable. Enjoy!

1

"Friendship is Love without his wings"

Lord Byron

(Painted in 2002 while holidaying at Gary and Sue's home in Quesnel, BC)

"The most essential thing for the gift of happiness is the gift of friendship"

Sir William Osler

(Painted in 1944 for my dear friend Winnie, whom you'll hear about in this story)

THIS STORY IS DEDICATED TO MY TWO PRECIOUS SONS,
GARY AND FRANCIS, WHO HAVE ENCOURAGED ME IN THIS PROJECT.

Gary John Graf   Francis Alexander Graf

A New Family Settles in America

1881 – 1912

Children Arrive and Grow in that New Family

1912 – 1930

A NEW FAMILY SETTLES IN AMERICA

1881 - 1912

The Palmer family in Southampton, England around 1890

From left to right
Kate, Mary, Charles (Dad), Emily Clara Agnes Mary (my paternal Grandma),
Bernard, Alfred James (my paternal Grandpa)
Francis (seated centre front)

My story begins in Southampton, England where Charles Palmer (my Dad), born
August 12, 1881 and baptized in the Roman Catholic church, attended a Catholic
boys' school and grew to become a handsome, debonair, artistic, adventurous,
scholarly mature man of 24 years. He had been attending college in Trafalgar
Square in London studying architecture & drafting. He was athletic, and played on
the college cricket team.

My Dad

One day in 1905, after cricket practice, he and the fellow team members were chatting and got on to the topic of immigration to America – that "land of milk and honey "with free land and wide open spaces as it was portrayed in all the college brochures and newspapers of the early 1900's.

Frank Woolliams and my Dad were in the pair that seemed to be gathering enthusiasm over the America idea.
Charlie, have you ever thought of taking a trip over to Canada?' queried Frank.

"Once in a while I do think it would be interesting. Just think of all that wide open space that could be ours if we did decide to stay" replied Charles.

Frank added " I'm ready for a change right now".
"Let's look into it, and see what it involves," said Charles.

When the college term ended the two were on their way to Canada.

They arrived in Harris, Sask. and C. G. Angell, a friend and homesteader, met them at the station with a wagon and a team of horses. The homestead was 13 ½ miles from Harris. The four homesteaders, Charles Palmer, Frank Woolliams, Cecil Angell, and Bruce Clegg had their four quarters of land in one section. While they built their sod houses in the four corners of that section, they lived in the sod house pictured below. Dad used to tell the story that for a sugar bowl they used a bowler hat jammed into the sod by the brim!

WOLLIAMS, PALMER & ANGELL SOD HOUSE 1905

The following letter describes very succinctly how these young men went about finding their homesteads. It was given to me, years ago, by Eldon Woolliams (an MP for Calgary- Bow River for 10 years) and written by his father, Frank Woolliams, one of the original three on the aforementioned cricket team. Below is a photo of Eldon. He passed this letter on to me several years ago.

7

Marriott P. O.
Sask, 23rd June, 1955

Dear Eldon:
 You will find enclosed, a brief summary of the 1st year on
the Prairie.
I read it over - one has to be in the mood to do this sort of
thing. Guess I was not in that mood. Destroy, or do what
you like with it, there is one thing if you keep it, it would
be a record.

Yours affectionately,

Dad

P. S. If I had put in all details in it would have been a
book.

It was the N. W. T. being made into the Province of
Saskatchewan that year. REMINISCENCES OF MY
HOMESTEAD DAYS IN THE YEAR 1905

I and two friends (Chas. L Palmer, and Cecil Angell)
homesteaded here on Sec. 14, T32, R14, W 3rd. We landed
in Saskatoon Mar. 14th, 1905, having come from Toronto
that spring. The spring was exceptionally early that year;
we stopped off in Winnipeg, the snow was all gone, the sun
quite warm, quite a change to the weather we left in
Toronto. Winnipeg had wood sidewalks, & old grass was
showing up between the boards, the streets were ankle deep
in mud. Travelling from Regina to Saskatoon, the train
had to stop to get up steam, we arrived Saskatoon dark at
night, a man ran up & down with a lantern, saying we
were at our destination; so we tumbled out, being a good 3
ft. from terra firma, being no station, or platform, that

8

side of river, a "Pile Bridge" across had been washed out that spring; for some reason the ferry was not used, so we had to board a boat & landed some distance downstream. Being dark, we could not see far. We eventually arrived at the Butler Hotel. The Hotel was full, so we slept in corridors, or anywhere we could find space to lay down, looking across the river next morning the only residence visible, was a plastered house, looking substantial on the bank; understood it had been Riel's residence. Saskatoon was quite a frontier Town with many tents here, and there; the sun was quite warm, shining brightly as it knows how to shine on the Prairies, the country looked dry and dusty with exception of low lying land & sloughs.

That day we visited the Government Land Office, a branch of the Govt. Office at Battleford. We had made inquiries in Winnipeg & were informed about Grand Trunk Railway, now the Canadian National, was surveyed south of Goose Lake, in a westerly direction; our idea was to get somewhere near that survey. In the Office was a lad whose people came out with the "Bar Colonists" 2 years before, he gave us lots of information on several sections of land open for filing in that direction; he also introduced us to a young man named Angus McMillan, whose business was to drive parties, of would be settlers, charging so much a head for locating. I might add here another young man, (Bruce Clegg) had asked to join our party, making 4 of us altogether.

We followed the Goose Lake or Bone Trail, named after the Indians, who had used it to haul Buffalo bones into Saskatoon, to be shipped to Chemical factories in the East. Settlers along the route had turned their temporary homes into stopping places where you could obtain meals & put up for the night, a distance of 50 to 60 miles out along this celebrated Bone Trail, after that it was the end of all habitations. These places extended west, as the years went on, as far as the Alberta Border, before the Calgary Railway went through. "Shells" about 30 miles out, was a well known stopping place, the company you would meet here were all grades of academic standing, many were debates, as to the future of this vast territory, carried on well into the night! Some of these places just sod, we laid on the floor if there was a floor, like sardines in the clothes you stood up in, often both sexes. There is no doubt large parcels of land changed hands at a profit to speculators & resold to the Homesteaders. We travelled round the East side of the Lake & south of Crystal Beach (known then as Devil's Lake) down as far as where Fortune is today.   It was somewhere in this area our 1st section was chosen; it was also here we drove around one section all hillocks, we passed this section up, too difficult to work. Probably this is one of the best wheat sections today, but we did not have the power. We stayed that night in a shack, near where Zealandia is today; Bartlett was the name of the settler; two of the party going some distance away to a settler who came from New Zealand. These settlers came out in the fall of 1904 & put the water in there. Zealandia is named after this man.

On the train coming up from Winnipeg, we had contacted young men from the States, who had been home for the winter,& coming back to complete their Duties: in conversation they told us what to avoid, when choosing our land, & whatever we did, avoid alkali. We drove down from here in a N. W. direction; crossing "Eagle Creek", we stripped and carrying our clothes on our backs crossed on foot, enabling Angus to drive the Democrat across without any difficulty. Here we sat on the bank in the sun & ate some lunch, it was real warm, we continued on into the district, to what is called the Marriott Municipality of today. I remember perfectly well the Prairie here was all burnt off & there was no habitation, here we chose a section no.14.   T32   R14.W3rd. This was our 4th choice & was the section we filed on; all the others had been filed on in our absence. This will give you a little idea of the rush for this land at that time.

On our return journey we crossed "Eagle Creek" just west and north of where the Town of Harris is today. An old couple named "Harris" had a stopping place; this was a roomy place, all built of sods, also a stable for our horses; here we stayed the night, again sleeping on the floor: I remember the old lady here so well; we boys pulled out a pack of cards to pass the time; she came to us and said she did not allow cards in her home; she was a kind old soul & did many little kindnesses for us boys in after years.

If you're ever out in the Harris, Sask. area you will find this memorial to mark the Harris Stopping Place on the Bone Trail 1904 - 09. I took this picture in 1985 when my brother Francis took us out to see it. On the next page is another view taken the same day. My brother, Francis, and his wife, Olive and my husband, John Graf are standing by the memorial. The ever present prairie wind is blowing as it can surely blow across those plains.

In the Harris Museum you will also find a one horse plough inscribed with the names Charles Palmer, Frank Woolliams, Cecil Angell in memory of these homesteaders.

Continuing Mr. Woolliams' letter..........

The night following, we stayed 15 miles from Saskatoon; this settler had followed a Circus all his life & was an interesting character. On arriving in Saskatoon, one of the boys (Palmer) found he had left his pocketbook under his pillow, so he borrowed a bicycle & rode back on the Goose Lake Trail & was fortunate to find it where he had left it. Previously the 3 of us had pooled all our money, the 4th, who had joined us in Saskatoon, financed his own expenses & decided to stay in Saskatoon until hearing from home.

We now got busy purchasing our supplies, having filed on our land, as it was our intention to start our duties immediately - that is, live 6 months in every year, for 3 years, & cultivate 30 acres of the land. There was quite a saying you bet the Government $10 against their 160 acres, for there were men who lost their deposit. The purchase of a team of oxen was our biggest outlay: we chose a team about 4 years of age, for symmetry of form & physique was all that one desired, of course the dealer said they were broken & we thought we had a bargain; our difficulties started before we got out of town, as they always wanted to go in the opposite direction to where you wanted to go & we got messed up in a slough, somewhere in one of the main avenues of today. At last we got on the trail, had not got far when they laid on the tongue of the wagon, putting a bow in it, that was there as long as we owned the wagon. We managed to get along a mile or two more & they ran into a poplar bluff from which we had to chop our way out; by this time seeing a small sized barn just off the Trail, investigated, finding nobody around, decided to camp for the night, lit a campfire, had supper & retired for the night after one of the boys had fallen through a trap door astride a stall; we were very comfortable in the hay stored here; understood this barn belonged to Caswell- was probably used to work some land from this point.

We were away early in the morning & with some difficulty managed to get a mile or two further; came across a small shack; here we tried to get some warm water for breakfast. A man came out & during our conversation we mentioned the difficulties with the oxen. (He was from the States), "Oh", he said. "They are not broken, no doubt just off the range. Get your plough out; I will help you break them in". Admit he did try, as far as I could see, made no progress except make a snake-like mark on the Prairie & it took all of us to handle the situation. A Buffalo trail would be much straighter, however it went towards his duties as he had no team. By this time we had decided to take them back to town & try to trade them off for another team. This was a wise decision, in Saskatoon we contacted a Doukhabor lad in his late teens who had a team for sale, after a little bartering he took our team & a few dollars in exchange & the deal was made. They were just the opposite to ours, one had a crumpled horn, the other a little undersized, one thing we noticed they were broken to the bit, like horses, & under perfect control; we tried them on the load, which they handled with ease, & from then on, had no trouble. A week had elapsed since we started, but time was what we had most of. We started again, all we had to do was tie the lines up, put them on the trail, wander around, shoot ducks & (prairie) chicken & when we camped, clean them out, cover with clay, put them in the fire, & when done, the clay & feathers all came away, leaving the meat inside delicious. We had a snow flurry one day, this did not stop our progress, in 24 hours it was all gone, the sun came out & our spirits rose with the sun, although reminding us, summer was not here yet. We slept under the wagon, laying a large canvas on the ground, rolling ourselves in blankets & pulling the canvas over us like a sleeping bag. This way we camped wherever place and circumstances suited us, following the bone trail for about 50 miles out of Saskatoon. The trail branched out in many directions, according to the way the settlers wanted to go.

One morning early we reached Harris's stopping place, here one trail went south, & another west, which we took; we stopped to have a chat & Mrs. Harris brought us each out a cup of steaming hot coffee- thus putting herself into our good graces for all time. We crossed Eagle Creek, just west of here, as before no bridges; another settler got stuck in the creek bottom. We hitched our oxen onto the end of the tongue & pulled him out; by this time we were getting proud of our oxen; after crossing Eagle Creek flat, we came out on to the high table land & came across 3 settlers like ourselves, who had the walls of a shack up but no roof on, one corner they had erected the stove & were making a stew, having shot a jack rabbit, they had dumplings & potatoes in the stew & they invited us to join them. It sure tasted good! We must have camped somewhere near here for the night; the next morning we took our bearings from the survey mounds & noted we had 10 miles to go straight

West. The sections' stake in N. E. corners had particulars in Roman figures showing section and picked out a suitable spot, close to a slough with water; the unburnt grass around the slough was rank, we immediately got out our breaking plow, plowed some sods dug into the ground about 3 ft. deep, 6 ft. wide, & 12 ft. long, built a wall of sods 3 to 4 ft. higher around the edge; used the lumber we had brought out for doors and windows, laid this on the top, pulling slough grass with our hands, & put over the roof, keeping it down with a thin layer of sods. We then filled our ticking we had brought with slough grass, laid our canvas on the ground inside, put our mattress we had made on top, & our bed was ready. The next thing, we erected the stove; the wagon box we turned upside down & put all our provisions and perishable goods inside; we also had brought out a wood oil barrel which we cut in half, one half we used as a table outside & the other half we had for a washtub. Cooking our supper, after which we lit our pipes, well satisfied with ourselves before going to bed under our own roof. The next day we measured up the land, to find the centre of section, there we placed a stone, also dug a well by the slough, this gave us soakage water for drinking and cooking purposes. The summer was spent building sod shacks on each quarter section.

In the centre this was known as the English village in after years as a trail went through the centre of shacks; we also built a barn for 8 head, a small chicken house & feed shed that year. We dug a proper well, went to Saskatoon for lumber for the curbing. We also put up stacks of hay, during this time many neighbours came in, one had a mower & rake, we paid him $6 a day to cut hay & rake it. Hay could be cut anywhere on a low piece of ground or slough as we had lots of rain that year. We had various adventures. After about 6 weeks the other lad came out with another team of oxen & a riding pony, also a tent, this we all used, until our shacks were completed. We all dined in one shack, taking a week on, each of us, to do the cooking. After the shacks were completed the tent was taken to Devil's Lake (Crystal Beach today) & erected by the Lake, where one would stay taking turns about, with both teams hauling wood for the winter. This was erected into timbers by the shacks for winter use.

We had many experiences during all this time; one thing I feel I must relate: A party of settlers, out locating; as I stated the trail went by the shacks, called the Rib Trail, a branch of the main trail, it was called the Rib Trail as we had stuck up a buffalo rib in ground to show where to turn off. This party had been indulging too freely with the bottle. We were all busy building the sod buildings at the time. I remember quite well one of us was holding the plow, one leading the oxen, as we had to have these sods exact, another cutting them in lengths with a spade. We stopped & had a little refreshments with them, they were quite jovial. During the coming winter a neighbour said he had a paper from home (North Dakota) & in it there was a jocular article about 3 green Englishmen plowing with 1 team of oxen. That spring we saw coming over the hill on our trail two 4-horse outfits loaded sky high with lumber, implements, etc., on arriving, we noticed it was the same party who were locating the summer before; they asked us to direct them to section 28; saying they had homesteaded that section & bought section 27. We knew this land was in the alkali area; one of the boys went with them to direct, they went down with their loads to the hubs & took them all day to get out, with our assistance, (Those that laugh last laugh longest!) We also plowed a fire guard round this section of ours-that is, we plowed a few furrows 2 rods apart, & burnt the grass off in the fall; This was necessary, as many prairie fires passed us during the early years.

By August we decided that 2 of us should go out harvesting whilst the other two stayed behind to look after the stock etc., A neighbour had been over (an American) to say he would like one of us to go with him & that he was thinking of walking south to Swift Current, by going east on the main line we would get to the harvest fields. We thought it a good idea, so we tossed up to see who should go with him. It fell to my lot. The other lad had some acquaintances at Indian Head & he went there later.

We left on Wed. the 2nd of Aug. 1905 taking with us our blankets, bread, tea, oatmeal, and off for Swift Current. I had a map I had bought in Saskatoon. We noted certain trails marked on it, so decided to walk west 'til we came to a trail made by the military in the "Riel Rebellion" to Battleford. Walking west, we crossed Prince Albert trail -S 31-T31-R 17 -W. of the 3rd. We crossed the creek on this trail to Swift Current, entering the Hills S. W. of Rosetown or where Rosetown is now. Here we laid down in our blankets, side of trail, covering our faces up; that night a band of Indians passed us; started walking again at daylight -- we struck no water that day, we passed the place where the Indians had camped, but no water; next morning we were desperate for water, I took my map out & noticed a small Lake marked about 3 miles west of us, so we decided to go our of our way for this water, when we got there, we were worse off than ever; yes, there was a little water in the centre, we could not reach, it would have taken us up to our hips in mud and slush & undoubtedly unfit to drink; so we retraced our weary steps back to trail. It was a fearfully hot day fortunately for us a thunderstorm came up & water ran down in pools in the trail. So this we strained through gravel, made tea & porridge, having carried small bits of trash, etc., for fire, as there was nothing but bald prairie in this vicinity.

As we continued another storm came up, so we took out the military survey rods (this trail was surveyed by the military) & made a sort of A-shape shelter, with our blankets, crawled under and went to sleep, being free from mosquitoes, whilst raining. This refreshed us considerably, it was 5 P. M. before we continued, walking till 10 P.M. it was quite dark; we made a smudge from trash we carried & what we could pick up around; we had also carried some

17

water; mosquitoes were our greatest trial. I put my hand at the back of my neck & when drawn away, would be covered in blood, we were also bothered with dysentry - evidently the water; we rested fairly good that night, felt refreshed the next morning & we continued on our journey.

Towards evening we came out of the hills & came to a depression or very wide gully. Thinking it was the river, we walked on & were very disappointed when we found we had travelled out of this, up on the Table land again: we were now getting anxious to reach the river & walked on well through the night, at last we laid down so tired & were soon asleep. Next morning the sun was away up when we awoke, quite refreshed & feeling better. Oh, what a blessing is sleep!! Had not walked far that morning, when we saw what we thought were shacks in the distance; there were also signs of animal life around. We walked on towards them, found they were tents belonging to the Matador Ranch, on a round-up of horses. Walking into the cook's tent, after being questioned & telling him who we were, he said the Boss is a good sort, was engaged at the moment with a buyer from Regina & would undoubtedly treat us right. This was only too true.

After a while he came up to us & said we could stay and rest & he would be driving into Swift Current in a day or two & take us with him. We found out we were 10 miles from Saskatchewan Landing. After a good meal, we laid down in the shelter of the chuck wagon & watched them cutting out horses from a large herd, must have been 2 or 3 thousand, all told there were about 10 cowboys, that night we went out with the night hawk - a lad in his late teens - his job was to look after the riding horses, about 80; we made a smudge, sat around holding bridles ready for any emergency. In the distance there were several bunches of horses.

The Foreman was a tall man about 6'6" - they called him "Legs" - he was a real he-man -kind & very efficient. We noticed every one of the cowboys looked up to him! He was from Texas & had what I call a beautiful drawl! The next morning I was to see him at work with the lasso; the lad whom we accompanied the night before, would ride these riding horses into a rope corral & if the cowboys had any difficulty getting their mounts, he would pick them out for them; never saw him miss a horse; he would then give them orders & make notes in a little book. One cowboy acted as scout & would ride away, probably be away 2 days & come back & report where the horses were to be found. We understood they moved camp accordingly.

A number of nationalities were represented, English, Canadian, American, half- breeds, & one from Australia. The cook was Irish, & at mealtimes the conversation was witty & humorous. Whilst there we had visitors from other ranches, some of the cowboys had small ranches of their own along the river & if a stray turned up, without a brand, they would put their own on, enabling them to build up quite a herd of their own.

One remark struck me very forcibly by one of these visitors to the man from Australia; "How would you like to go down the Strand?" meaning London, Eng. The contrast to me was so apparent. There was a little exhibition riding to the benefit of buyer from Regina; one of the half-breeds gave a wonderful display of horsemanship. We had a front seat & saw it all. The day came when they decided to drive the horses purchased to Swift Current & load them in railway cars. Everybody was moving around early. We were asked to take a team & wagon to Saskatchewan Landing where one of the boys would take it over & bring back a load of wood for cook wagon. The Boss said he would pick us up there & take us the rest of the way to Swift Current. On arriving at river everything was ready for fording. The cowboys sat their horses proudly with the horses purchased, surrounded at the edge of the river. The scene was picturesque, as their shirts clean with bright colors & Bull Durham tags hanging out of their hip pockets. It was a work of art to see them make a cigarette on their restless horses. To add to the picture the Indians who had passed us on the trail were camped in their teepees by the river. Close by antelope could be seen grazing on the top of the hills rising up on the other side.

Soon after our arrival the orders were given to ford the river, one of their number had been lassoed & pulled into the river, the others were crowded after it, a good 100 of them, possibly more & they swam across coming out on the other side. A halt was made here at a ranch house & everybody had   their dinner. I remember one of the cowboys, taking his mount out of the Barn here, it got loose & immediately began to clear all humans out of the Barn. I climbed the partition just in time.

That was the last I saw of them; we then got up in democrat with Boss & buyer, it was dark on arriving in Swift Current, although the team never let up all the way, My chum and I parted here. He decided to go on to Regina with the horses. I decided to jump a freight & go on to Moose Jaw. I caught a freight that night, got in a boxcar full of lumber.

I lay down & went clean off to sleep- the next thing I remember much about was being planted in Moose Jaw freight yards. Here I stayed all fall putting up hay, stooking, threshing. I put in 40 days threshing with a steam outfit belonging to a man named Rathwell, who had put up as a Conservative in our new Provincial House. He lost out. I think his opponent was Ross (Liberal). Mr. Rathwell had a large family of sons who managed the farm. Their land covered a large area - a little broken on each parcel of land.

We were very comfortable at the Home Farm sleeping in a large Barn. After a time, we moved around the country doing threshing for his neighbors, where we slept in straw piles & behind our horses. Some crops had been hailed. Evidently he wanted to be a good Conservative, as he could not have made anything out of these neighbors.

We had a bad snow storm about the 20th Oct. This laid us up for the rest of the month. The snow all went & we had Indian summer through November & we did lots of stook threshing. After that we finished up early in December stook threshing near the Barn, in a blizzard! Needless to say I had become very tough.

I returned home via Regina by train to Saskatoon. I remember the wooden sidewalks in Regina, also N. W. M.P. Barracks. On arriving in Saskatoon, a near neighbor was in & I had a lift out to the Homestead. My chum was pleased to see me. He had been into Saskatoon, got a load of provisions for the winter with the money I had sent him & I landed with about a hundred $ in my pocket. As my wages at the highest was only $2 a day, I thought I had done well. After my arrival we took our guns and went N. W. to what we called 60 mile Bush. There were several ranchers there, one we became acquainted with called "Montana Bill". He had a bunch of cattle and was killing them off for the settlers. We bought several quarters of Beef @ 6 cents per lb. The other lad who went to Indian Head did not come home but worked his way to the coast & got a job on a cattle boat & went to England returning in the spring. Thus ended the first year of our Homesteading. The worst of the winter we spent visiting neighbors, playing bridge, reading and writing letters home. The following year brought more adventures, hard work, but that is another story. This reminds me of a verse I learned as a boy:

"The human will, that force unseen,

The offspring of a deathless soul,

Can hew a way to any goal,

Though walls of granite intervene".

Yours sincerely
Frank Woolliams

Charles Lewis Palmer, Homesteader, 1905.

Dad made two trips back to England. In 1909 he gave Gladys Molyneux, his sweetheart (only 17 yrs. old) a beautiful solitaire diamond ring. They planned to marry in two years when he would return to England to get her.

I presented that ring with "The story of the Ring" to my darling oldest grand-daughter, Marnie Graf, in June, 1996 on the occasion of her Grade 12 graduation from Quesnel Secondary School.

Registration District South Stoneham

1892. Birth in the Sub-District of Millbrook in the County of Southampton

No.	1 When and Where Born.	2 Name, if any.	3 Sex.	4 Name and Surname of Father.	5 Name and Maiden Surname of Mother.	6 Rank or Profession of Father.	7 Signature, Description and Residence of Informant.	8 When Registered.	9 Signature of Registrar.	10 Baptismal Name, if added after Registration of birth.
80	Twentieth September 1892 Hb Millbrook Road Freemantle Millbrook UsB	Gladys Dorothy	Girl	Samuel Molyneux	Annie Mary Molyneux formerly Hearl	of Independent Means	S. Molyneux Father Hb Millbrook Road Freemantle Millbrook	Tenth November 1892	Charles Stewart Registrar.	

I, BRUCE ELLERY, Superintendent Registrar for the District of SOUTHAMPTON, in the County of Southampton do hereby certify that this is a true copy of the Entry No. 80 in the Register Book of Births No. 40 for the above-named Sub-District, and that such Register Book is now legally in my custody.

WITNESS MY HAND this 1st day of June, 1949.

CAUTION.—Any person who (1) falsifies any of the particulars on this Certificate, or (2) uses it as true, knowing it to be falsified, is liable to Prosecution.

Bruce Ellery
Superintendent Registrar.

Above is a copy of my mother's birth certificate.

In Southampton, England there arrived a beautiful little baby girl, Gladys Dorothy Hall Molyneux, born on September 20, 1892 . She grew to have glossy black wavy hair and a bubbly personality – the joy of her father's heart - (note the photo of Gladys and her father, taken in 1898, in the first car on a Southampton street) Her mother had died when she was an infant. She was baptized in the "High Anglican" church. A "governess" looked after her daily needs, and she had a tutor to teach her school lessons. Gladys was athletic and energetic – loved tennis, rollerskating, and dancing. She was a bright student with a particular interest in the French language as I found out later when I was studying my high school French by correspondence - Mother was always eager and able to help.

This is Mother, taken in 1898, when she is 6 years of age. She is having a ride with her father, my maternal Grandpa Molyneux, in his new car – the first car to arrive in Southampton, England. Just imagine what excitement that caused! This is the only photo I have of my Grandfather Molyneux. Mother brought it from England in her steamer trunk of treasures.

Mother's Dad died when she was only 14 years of age. Then she went to live with her brother, Louis, in the above home until, at 19, she came to Canada to live in a sod house. Quite a change!

This is Mother taken before she and Dad were married. She is costumed in her older sister's nursing uniform all set for date to go to a skating carnival with Dad. Below is what was written on the back of the Postcard. She wrote *"This is how C and I went to a skating carnival, he is behind in the*

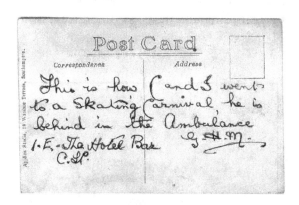

ambulance." Dad wrote *"I.E. The Hotel Bar ".C.L.P.*

This is the only sample I have of my Dad's handwriting.

Mother's oldest sister, Annie, with her maid. This is the one and only picture I have of any of Mother's siblings. Aren't the hats gorgeous?

Dad's sister, my Auntie Mary, and husband Charles Barlow. These are the parents of my dear cousin Clare Hayward whom I have corresponded with since I was ten years old and have visited three times in Southampton, England.

For a moment I will draw your attention to my childhood diary in the January 17th entry for 1936 which is on the next page - *I received a letter from the old country today, from my cousin Clare.* I was eleven years old when I wrote that in my childhood diary.

Back to my story about my parents –

Mixed religion marriages were not allowed in the Roman Catholic Church in those days, so Gladys and Charles had to get a dispensation from the Pope before the ceremony would be allowed. This they secured and my mother married my father on January 31, 1912 in St. Edmunds' RC Church in Southampton, England.

I have had the privilege of attending Mass there three times – in 1972, 1992, and in 2000. What a joy to walk down the aisle of the church where my parents received that marriage blessing that was to carry them through 39 years of marriage! Some of the ups and downs of those years I will tell you about in this story. On the next page is a copy of their marriage as recorded in the archives of the church. A dear priest found it for me in the church archives on one of my visits to Southampton, and also presented me with a souvenir booklet of the church's centenary which has the sketch of the church shown below on its front cover.

My husband, John Weicker, with cousin Clare & Roy in front of St. Edmund's Church, Southampton, England in 2000.

Another view of St. Edmund's Church where my parents were married in 1912. We attended Mass here in 2000 when we spent a week in Southampton visiting Brighton, the Isle of Wight and other places my parents talked about.

Here is the going away photo of Gladys and Charles (now Mr. & Mrs. Charles Palmer), full of the love of adventure, excited about starting life in this vast new continent and country.

Charles had booked passage on the fateful Titanic, all set to sail on April 12, 1912 but Gladys happened to let slip, in a casual conversation, that she had, while Charles was in Canada, gone on a couple of dates roller skating and dancing with the First Officer of the Titanic. Immediately, when Charlie heard this, he said "No way am I having one of the ship's crew making eyes at my bride on our honeymoon!" Consequently he cancelled those reservations and booked passage on the Mauritania - I think – I'm not absolutely certain of this because I recall Mother told me they came over on the Acquitania, but when I looked into this when in

Southampton Titanic Museum in 2000 I was told that the Acquitania did not take passengers, but it would have been the Mauritania. I have as yet not been able to locate a passenger list for that April voyage.

Both Gladys & Charles's parents had died before they married, but Gladys said good-bye to a brother, Louis, and two sisters, Valerie and Anne Marie. Charles left behind brothers Francis, Frederick, Alfred, Bernard, Kathleen and Mary. One brother, who was also an architect, came to Canada, settled in Vancouver and designed one of the Catholic churches at the beginning of the century. I have tried to track down which one but so far no luck. My Mother never saw her siblings again as she never went back to England, nor did Dad, except for the Vancouver brother with whom they kept in touch for several years but then heard no more and they seemed to lose track of one another.

Here are the newly weds! Dad had this cozy sod house all ready for his bride – this was taken in the winter of 1912. They did spend a month that winter in Vancouver probably spending time with my uncle and his wife, although we children never did meet this family. I do faintly remember parcels of candy used to arrive at Christmas from our "coast relatives" – that's all I can remember about them.

Mother always spoke boastfully about their sod house in that it had a "lumber roof" - I guess many of the sod houses of that time had the roofs of sod. As you will have noticed on the previous page 7 the first one that Dad, Frank Woolliams, and Cecil Angell lived in was very primitive. No wonder that Dad 's lungs got weakened and left him susceptible to TB in later years.

Mum & Dad's neighbours all contributed to a wedding gift for them – a mantel clock purchased from the T. Eaton Co. by catalogue. That clock rested on the piano in our home on the farm, was brought to B.C. when my parents moved to Kelowna in 1949. Mother later presented it to me and I gave it to my son, Francis, on his 40th birthday in 1996. Francis has had the clock completely restored and now it proudly chimes out the hours on his parlour mantel in Victoria, BC.

The first crops Dad hauled to Saskatoon (75 miles) were with oxen and took a week. How lonely it must have been for Mother to wait for his return! He would then arrive home with enough flour to last the winter and supplies you couldn't grow, such as sugar, tea and kerosene. The farm was as close to self-sufficient as could be. Dad worked in the fields and barns. Mother (this 19 yr. old bride) learned very quickly how to cook and do canning, keep a big garden, and make bread.

Then along came the babies. My oldest sister, Margaret, was born in 1913, and died at three months of age. To lose a baby one has held in your arms is terrible. Tragedies like these were all too common in these early settlers' lives. The nearest doctor was in Harris which was 13 ½ miles away, so mid-wives attended births. I remember my Mother attending two of her friends having their babies even in the late 1920's.

On July 4,1914 along came my sister, Gladys.

On Dec.4, 1915 Francis arrived, then Bernard on May 3, 1919.

Here they are – Gladys, Bernard and Francis – a darling threesome who pampered their animals, loved to roam and frolic on the wide open prairie spaces. Mum and Dad were so happy - the crops were good, the children were healthy, intelligent and growing fast. Mum was enjoying learning from her pioneer neighbours all the tricks of gardening, canning, cooking, sewing and being the wife of a homesteading farmer. In fact they managed (with the help of an inheritance for Mother) to buy a new Overland car and the quarter of land that Cecil Angell put up for sale as he and his family were moving closer to Harris and later to Saskatoon. The farm life was not for his wife, Maude. But Mother missed Maude when she moved away – they remained lifelong friends. Gertrude Woolliams and Mother didn't hit it off – spent more time being miffed at each other than communicating. What a shame! As Sybil (Gerty's daughter and I have said – What a waste!) Woolliams quarter was right next to ours.

Following is another photo of the "threesome". One can just imagine how they loved roaming across the half section – chasing gophers, picking crocuses-those beautiful mauve flowers that were so welcome in the early days of May, and finding Indian arrowheads. The latter were quite a common treasure to find when walking in our pasture and were quite a work of art, I realize now when I don't have any of them.   We didn't value them when we were children- they were so common. After all, as you perhaps noted in Frank Woolliams letter – the Indians were camped on our quarter section just previous to our parents settling there.

Crocuses (watercolour pencil I painted in 2000), as we found them in our pasture when I was a child.

I remember my childhood as being free of the concerns of the larger world. To quote Lorraine Bashi in her "Growing up in Western Canada" *Our world was our neighbourhood, our community - a familiar and unthreatening place, while every other place in the world was remote and undefined. We remember a time when we could play and feel safe in doing so, out of sight of parents or other adults.*"

postcard photo of prairie crocuses

Francis, Gladys, and Bernard (before I was born – they were probably ages 8, 9, and 4 years of age.

We can just picture these three riding horses, running and jumping, chasing each other and their cats, dogs, horses and cows - just having lots of fun on the wide open spaces of their prairie farm, then returning to the home kitchen – warm & glowing, smelling of Mother's newly baked bread and "sugar cookies."

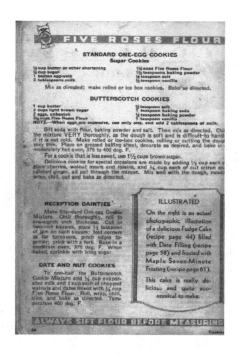

Mother's sugar cookie recipe from her favourite old Five Roses cookbook.

The three would then go upstairs to pursue their favourite hobbies while waiting for their supper - Gladys would do some art – she had a particular talent for drawing horses, Francis would be trying out some new card tricks, and Bernard would be planning the next cupboard he would construct - he loved helping his Dad with carpentry and from bits of boards and boxes would make cupboards for Mum and Mrs.Wilson (our closest neighbour). Sometimes they would have a puppet show with the jointed puppets that Dad carved in his spare time and put on strings for them to create their own shows.

As children's laughter rippled down from the upstairs bedroom Dad could be heard calling "Gladys, Francis, Bernard come here right away!"

Of course the three rushed downstairs to answer their Father's urgent call. They knew by his voice he meant business.

"Bernard, you are to go over to Mrs. Wilson's right away, and Gladys & Francis, you are to stay overnight at Woolliams's as your Mother & I want to be alone tonight. So off the children went, asking no further questions – you just didn't ask my Dad "Why do we have to do this?"
If we did he would just say "Because I told you to!"
So away scurried the children. In the meantime Dad said to Mother " Will you be alright until I get back?"
"Oh, yes, but hurry as fast as you can – I don't think it will be too long now."

Dad then drove our Overlander car to get Mrs. Weldwood, the district midwife to be with Mother. No doctors were present for births in those days. Mother had been with three of her friends to help them through their childbirths. Those pioneer ladies helped each other when needed.

My siblings were all born in the sod house but by the time I arrived we were living in a wood framed house.

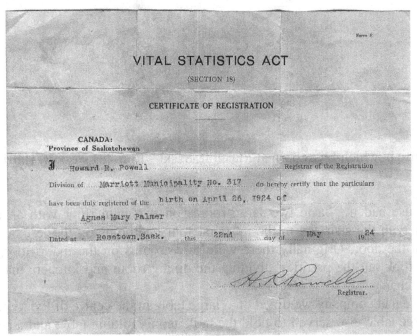

my original birth certificate

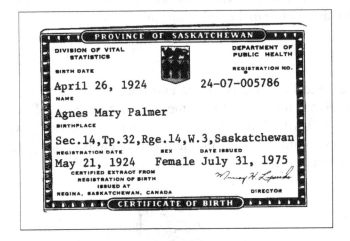

the plasticized copy I ordered and received in 1975

The house in which I was born at Marriott, Sask. - 13 miles west of Harris.

This house had the basic two large rooms on the main floor with an entrance hallway with the stairway to the upstairs' four bedrooms on the left side as you came in the door. Originally there were three rooms on the main floor, but my parents took out the partition dividing the dining room and kitchen, making one large kitchen.

When we had company we dined on a large table in the centre of the living room. This large table also served to hold the table tennis folding table and a pool table when we wished to play ping- pong. My parents believed in having all kinds of recreation available at all times. In the summer time we had a tennis court in our yard beside the house. In the winter months we hauled water from our well and flooded the tennis court to make a skating rink.

Mother was an excellent tennis player and after they acquired a car she would often drive to Harris for tennis tournaments and often win. Dad was a cracker-jack pool and billiard player. I remember many gatherings with friends and neighbours who would come to our house for tennis, pool games and skating parties in the winter time.

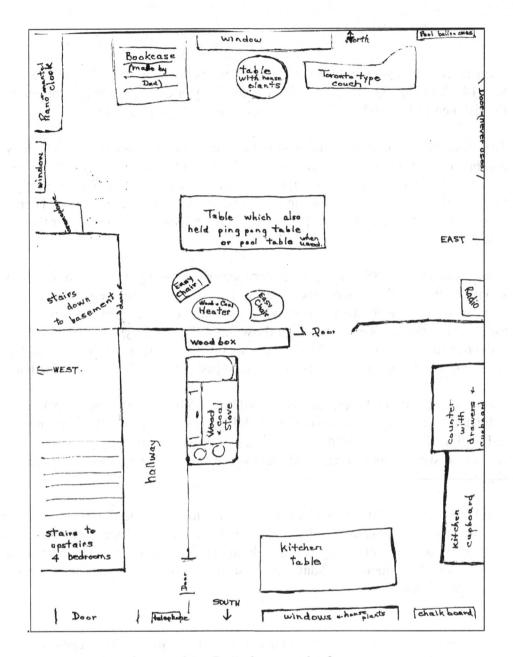

The floor plan of my home where I was born on the farm

I was born in the evening on April 26, 1924, in our home as described above – Sec. 14, Township 32, Range 14, West of the 3rd Meridian - that very spot that the Englishmen had picked out for their future homes 20 years previous!

My sister, Gladys tells me that the next morning Mrs. Woolliams said to Gladys and Francis and her own two - Sybil (age 11) and Eldon (age 9) they could walk over to Palmers for there was a surprise waiting for them. These four promptly ran the half-mile, into the house, up the stairs, and into Mum's bedroom. There I was – a new little sister for the Palmer children, and another playmate for the Woolliams!

Gladys (who is now 88, and although her memory is failing) says she remembers so vividly the day I was born when she was rushed away to the neighbours. Only 10 years old, she really didn't know what was going on – sex and births were not topics of discussion or explanation in those days. For all they knew babies arrived in the midwife's little black bag. However, when Gladys viewed that dear wee baby sister, she said she was so ecstatic – just what she had always wanted!

"Never again", says Gladys," did I play with my dolls, for now I had a real, live baby doll to dress up, push around in my doll carriage." Indeed, that's what she did – all my life she has been a very special sister and as my story goes on I will recall how she has always regarded me (even at 79 years of age) as her "little" sister."

Sybil (who lives in Palo Alto, CA is now 90, and memory and thinking is as sharp as it was when she was my teacher - the best I ever had) said she also remembers that day when they went to see this new little one. To add to the excitement, I was born on Mrs. Woolliams' birthday! Because of that Sybil's mother and I always had a special bond.

Eldon's comment was "Just look at those hands, all curled up, like puppy's paws!" He told me this many times, and again the last time I visited him in Calgary four years ago.

As far as I was told there were no comments from my brother, Francis, upon my arrival – he probably thought "Just another pesky little sister to tease!" Francis was always full of mischief and did love to tease me as the years went by.

Bernard probably just smiled in his wise and kindly way and kissed both Mother and baby on the cheeks.

Certificate of Baptism

This is to Certify *that* _Agnes Mary_

Child of _____

born on the _26th_ *day of* _April_ 19 _24_ *at* _Valley Centre_

was **BAPTISED** *on the* ___ *day of* ___ 19 _24_ *at* ___

ACCORDING TO THE RITE OF THE ROMAN CATHOLIC CHURCH

by the Rev. _Father N. J. McMillan_

Sponsors, _____
Lelia Russel

as appears from the Baptismal Register of Said Church.

_____ 19 _4 2_ _____ PASTOR

F. J. Tonkin Co. Ltd. Winnipeg   Approved Form No.

As this certificate states, I was baptised by Father McMillan on June 6th at Valley Centre. You will read later in my story why I needed to have this certificate in 1942 so was able to get it from St. Ann's church at Delisle, SK.

I have only this one baby picture of myself – perhaps my parents were now too busy with four lively children, to take pictures. I soon became an active member of the Palmer family, although I couldn't always keep up to my older brothers and sister in their hikes and rambling across the miles of our farm land.

Later it was to prove a blessing that I was not always with the others on their outings. Gladys did push me for many a mile in that pram and in her doll carriage.

One afternoon in early June the Saskatchewan countryside was especially beautiful with green grass appearing beside the roadway and new young leaves quivering and shining in the sunlight as it filtered through the bluffs of trees. Buds on the caragana bushes that edged our driveway were swelling, and sprouts were appearing in the huge that our parents planted to keep us in vegetables for the long winter months. A meadowlark was singing with liquid fluency in the pasture as Gladys, Francis, and Bernard set out on a usual walk.

I had been put upstairs in my crib for my regular afternoon nap with bedroom window wide open. Mother believed babies should have all the fresh air possible to store up in their young lungs, and was happy to see the other children with plans for the afternoon.

She called out to the children "Where are you going?"
"Just over to play with the Sinclair kids for an hour or so. Is that okay?" asked Gladys.
 "That's just fine," said Mother, "I'll phone Mrs. Sinclair and check first that it's fine with her." She went in to the front hallway and cranked on the phone in the front entrance (one with the crank on the side and bells on the front as illustrated on the next page).

41

Wall phone typical of those on farms

Sinclairs also had children of similar ages. One – Grace is now 95 and lives in Kyle Health Care nursing home where my sister lives.

Mrs. Sinclair said "That's great! Your children and ours always get along well together and seem to find plenty to amuse themselves. It's such a pleasantly warm day they will be able to play outside for the whole time".

Across the pasture they went, across the fields for approximately 3 ½ miles, arriving at the Sinclair farm. Grace, Donalda, Ken, Lil, and Pete – what fun to have all these kids to play with! They played ball for awhile, then were so hot one of them said "Let's take our shoes off and go for a dip in the dug-out."
"Good idea!" screamed the others and off they went for another ½ mile to a sloping, well-built dug-out of dammed up creek water that the Sinclairs had for watering their cattle. In jumped the children - remember these children had probably never seen open water - only creeks which were just shallow, gently flowing streams.

Oooh! That cool, sparkling water felt so refreshing. How the eight of them jumped and splashed until the mud was getting stirred up and the bottom could no longer be seen.
Little by little they spread out.

The children's shouting and laughter was suddenly interrupted by screams for "Help!"

Disaster had struck – the three Palmer Children had slipped into 8 ft. of water - the deepest centre of the dugout!! Bernard had sunk, then floated up and caught Gladys by the hair, pulling her in, and Francis was struggling to pull out his sister and little brother. Spluttering and screaming, Francis and Gladys were out but Bernard was still in the water and nowhere to be seen. The children ran for help.

Sybil tells me that when Bernard died my parents had just bought the new Overlander so Dad and Mother and Mr. Woolliams drove over to Sinclairs'. Parents quickly arrived on the scene. Artificial respiration was given to Bernard for over half an hour but to no avail. Our dear little eight year old, Bernard , all smiles and brightness and such a sweet, sunny nature, was dead.

Mrs. Woolliams walked across a newly ploughed field to be with Mother, and help look after the baby (me). Eldon and Sybil walked over to Palmers.

Sybil and Ben MacLeod (who was Bernard's best friend and is now 85 and living in Rosetown) tell me that Bernard's funeral Mass was attended by everyone of our friends and neighbours for miles around. The Muirland school children formed an honour guard and the Roman Catholic priest gave a moving eulogy. This must have been some comfort to Mother for after Bernard's death she converted to the R.C. church.

Dad seemed quite bitter toward the church for years after this disastrous happening – perhaps he couldn't understand how God could take away such a beautiful little child whom everyone loved so much. However, I can always picture Dad kneeling backwards into his easy chair to say his prayers before going upstairs to bed, and he did return to the church in his last years of life when living in Rutland, BC and it seemed to be a great joy to him. Religion was not something he discussed with us children – although we were all baptized into the RC faith, he never taught us prayers or told us Bible stories and there was no RC church within 20 miles. At Mother's knee we learned a little prayer as follows:

> Gentle Jesus meek and mild
> Look upon a little child
> If I should die before I wake
> I pray my soul The Lord to take.

(I'm not so sure this was a really relaxing thought to send one off to sleep!!) but probably one taught Mother by her governess.

Although I was just three years old at the time I will always remember the sadness and grief that hung like a cloud over our home for a long time. I was told that my dear little brother had "died and gone to heaven" So I used to lay on my back out in the middle of our pasture, look up at the cloud formations in the vast prairie sky and pick out formations that I would imagine as Bernard floating by.

Mrs. Wilson, when I visited her, as I often did, would point out to me the little cupboard she had that Bernard had made for her. She said she would keep it forever as a special memento.

Mother would, once in a while, invite me to come upstairs to her bedroom. She would then reach into the night table (which Bernard had made) beside her bed and take out this pretty box. In it she had some very special keepsakes. There she would, with tear filled eyes, show and explain to me – Bernard's glasses, his report card, a lock of his shiny, black hair, and other precious articles. She planted a special little round garden of flowers beside our house which was always referred to as "Bernard's garden". When John and I went back to Sask. in 1991 I took John to visit the site of our farm home. Although the buildings were no longer there, we did find the original trees and a little patch of flowers bravely blooming forth in "Bernard's garden" spot. What a symbol of memories that can never be taken away!!

One of the happy highlights of my third year of life was the arrival of Ginger whom we called "Ginn" for short. Ginn was a fluffy ginger-coloured kitten who soon became a much loved member of our family. I spent every spare hour I could petting her, dressing her in doll clothes and pushing her around in my doll carriage. I later found out that Ginn was a boy cat who took to wandering far afield every once in a while – looking for a girl friend no doubt, but as for me – I always used the pronouns "she" and "her" whenever I spoke about Ginn, and I loved that cat very much.

Ginn lived to the ripe old age of 16 years (that's really old for a cat). She became such a "people cat". If the door between our living room and the kitchen happened to be closed and Ginn was in the living room hoping to get into the kitchen where the rest of the family happened to be, she would climb up on the back of the easy chair, reach out, rattle the doorknob thereby letting us know that she was there and wanted to join us in the kitchen. Perhaps my family felt that this darling little kitten would help to lessen the sadness we all felt with the loss of my dear little brother.

Ginn and Dad

My childhood memories of life spent on the farm are mostly very happy ones. It was a great place to roam about with all the possibilities and wonders of life right there. Even though I had no-one of my age living nearby for the first eight years of my life, I learned to keep myself amused with playing with Ginn and my dolls, fashioned a little space out under the trees as a play house, and in the evenings did lots of drawing and painting by the light of the gas and kerosene lamps while Mum and Dad read, listened to the radio or played cards. Gladys and Francis were so much older and had other interests.

Francis, Gladys and I on horseback.

Notice the ringlets, and the saddle. I never did have a saddle when I rode horseback later to school and to the United Church Sunday School at Muirland School.

When I reached the age of six, our neighbour, Lil Wilson gave birth to a baby girl, Leona. I was delighted and spent many afternoons going over there to take the baby for a ride in her carriage until she was old enough to play with, then along came her baby sister, Elaine, so now I really had some playmates!

Wheat was the main crop on our farm, but we had a few cows, pigs, and chickens, with horses to pull the farm machinery. We were fortunate our soil was not full of stones as some fields were. We did not have to pick rocks as some farm families did farther south . My stepfather, Dick Leeks, had callouses on his hands from all the rocks he had to pick for many years on his homestead at Eatonia, Sask.

Because I was the baby of the family I realize now that I was quite "spoiled". On the farm there were always chores that belonged just to my older brother and sister, Gladys and Francis. There was wood and kindling to be chopped and carried in, water to be brought in and slops to be carried out to the pigs. Cows had to be milked and chickens had to be fed. Fresh straw bedding had to be put in the stalls. I was glad when the aroma of fresh straw outdid the other smells emanating from the cows and horses' stalls. Those stalls had to be cleaned daily –the smell of hot horse dung was not pleasant.. Chickens were not my favourite – they pooped everywhere and the chicken house also had a smell I hated – feathers and poop!! Gathering the eggs was fun but those chickens would wander and sometimes you'd find eggs in the hardest places to find and often way behind the barn in the hay stacks.

Here we see Gladys and Francis as they finish up the evening farm chores.

We always had two big gardens because they were our major source of food for both summer and winter. In the spring Mother and Dad planted the gardens. Mum let me plant some of the biggest seeds like the peas and corn but she was always close by making sure I did it right. In the summer the weeding (by hand) and hoeing had to be done – and in the fall all the root vegetables had to be dug up and put in storage in our basement. Fresh sand had to be hauled in which the carrots were buried. We all slept on straw mattresses that had to be filled with fresh straw when the harvesting was completed – oh that beautiful aroma of the fresh straw made up for the scratchiness which was there until you got it all hollowed out to smoothly fit your body. Gladys and I slept together until I left home to go to teacher training.

Gladys & I and one of our favourite calves.   My brother, Francis & Buster

Growing up on a farm, I got to care for and become fond of some of the animals. Beside Ginn, my cat, we always had a dog to keep me company when I went for long walks in the pasture or played by myself in my playhouse which was quite a distance from our house. Mother always had such a fear of losing me after the terrible loss of Bernard. She told me the following story years later.

One summer afternoon the wide open prairie grain field quivered shining and fragile in the sunlight. The blossoms on the caragana hedge nodded in the breeze and a redwinged blackbird sang with liquid fluency from the poplar trees just north of our house. The fragrance of the lemon pies in the oven filled the kitchen and drifted out the door.

Lemon Pie (Mum)
Juice of 2 lemons
2 cups sugar
Yolks of 3 eggs
4 tbsp. flour
Piece of butter
Stir all together with a little cold water.
Add 3 cups boiling water & bring to a
boil. Remove from stove & put in
baked crusts. This will make
2 pies.

Mother's recipe as I copied it in 1947

Mother's lemon pies were a masterpiece (that's why lemon pie to this day is my favourite). I was about 4 years old, playing out in the yard. I had wandered off into the field of grain on the quarter right south of our house. We had a bumper crop that year and the grain was over my head in height so Mother stepped out on the front steps just to check on my whereabouts. I was nowhere in sight.

Panicking, Mother anxiously called "Agnes, where are you?"
A tiny voice would reply "Here he is!" Mother would locate me by that sound and just hug and hug me to her heart. She said this happened more than once – I gather it became a game after that.

Back to my love of the animals – the horses all knew their names and would come when you called out to them. They knew you would have a handful of oats or a bundle of grass for them to munch on. Horses can be very faithful friends and they can also have a mind of their own.

I remember the day Buster, one of our horses of the set of six that Dad was using to pull the disk when he was preparing the soil for planting in the spring, stepped back and cut his leg just above the hoof on the back. It was a very deep cut. There were no veterinarians within hundreds of miles in those days. I remember vividly how Mother and Dad tried to stop the bleeding (they packed the wound with bandages made of clean white flour bags and sheets) but to no avail. Buster bled to death. What a sad time for us! Many tears were shed and our poor Dad had to find a special place and dig a very deep grave for Buster.

Gladys and Buster

My Diary

JANUARY 1

19**36** Sailor is sick, lovely
weather, above zero, been out
sliding, radio is good, stay
up late.

19**37** Today is New Year's Day.
We had a nice turkey meal.
It is quite frosty today. School
starts on Monday.

19**38** Today is New Year's Day.
Am quite tired from dance last
night. Very nice day today.

19**39** Jean Ritchie came over
to see me. We had a
good visit. Very cold.

19**40** We celebrated our New
Years' yesterday because Alex
was up. Mrs Wilson over. I
did some homework.

49

Once again I draw your attention to my childhood diary. I notice the very first entry on January 1, 1936 I wrote *Sailor is sick. Lovely weather, above zero. Been out sliding, radio is good, stay up late.*

I must explain -" Sailor" is one of our horses. You can see what was uppermost on my eleven year old mind on that New Year's Day.

The farm animals became our friends – even the pigs for you could not feed and care for them day after day and not get attached to a special one. But we had to learn not to be too sentimental about our animals. Unfortunately those same pigs and steers had to be slaughtered, butchered and served up on the dinner table at a later date. I took no part in the slaughtering and stayed far away from the butchering but soon forgot the source of those delicious roasts when their aromas reached us from the kitchen oven.

When a chicken dinner was planned or chicken soup was to be on our menu it did not mean a trip to the supermarket. In those days there were no supermarkets – we had a tiny store (owned & operated by Layton M. Angus) at Marriott (a siding) where the train came through – going south on Fridays, and returning north on Saturdays. But that store was our Post Office and sold only canned goods, cheese, jam, tea and coffee. The OK economy store in Rosetown stocked more fresh products, but we never got to Rosetown very often in those days – after all it was 17 miles away and money for gasoline was scarce. To get that chicken Mother or Dad (most often Mother because Dad would be out in the field) would go out in the chicken yard, catch the doomed hen or rooster , grab it by the neck and twirl it around about six times, then lay it on a chopping block out behind our house and off they'd chop its head.   It would then be brought in to the kitchen counter, cleaned and plucked (us kids all helped in this process) ready for stuffing to be roasted or into the pot to be boiled for soup (depending on the age of the bird).

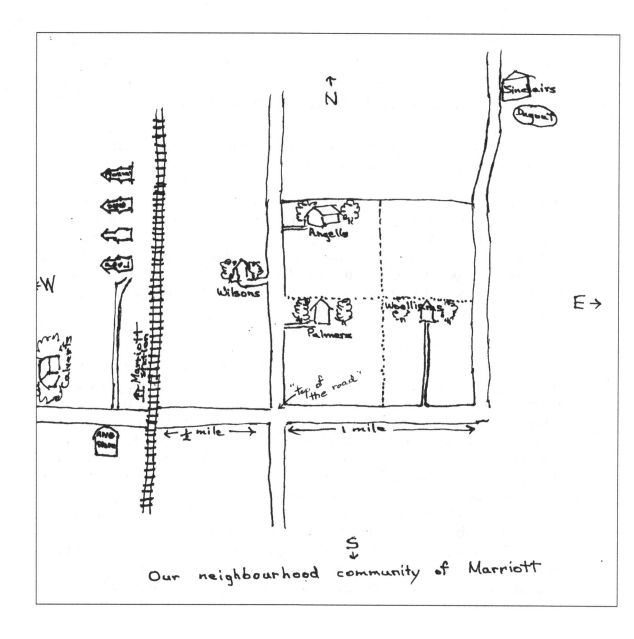

Our neighbourhood community of Marriott

So it was on the farm – everything we ate was produced right there except sugar, tea, coffee, flour, and oatmeal. We had friends from Saskatoon, the Dobsons, and the Adams family who would come out to visit us about once a year. They brought a gift box of groceries. I can recall even now the sweet taste and pungent aroma of those "store bought" jams, and boxed cereal. We only ever had oatmeal porridge and as a child I hated it – now I think it's delicious. Perhaps that's just because I was told I had to eat it "to grow up to be a big girl."

that's me - probably about 5 years of age

My years to Adulthood

1930 - 1941

MY YEARS TO ADULTHOOD

1930 – 1941

In April of 1930 I was very excited with thoughts of all the possibilities and wonders of life lying just around the corner with the starting of school. I wanted to be able, as were my older sister and brother, Gladys and Francis, to read, do homework, and most important of all, make new friends.

But my entry into formal schooling was delayed by a year.

One frosty Monday morning Mother and I hauled in buckets of snow and put them in the aluminum boiler on top of the wood stove so that the snow would melt and create a boiler full of beautifully soft water. The water from our well would be so hard and full of minerals that the soap would not produce the whitest wash. In the summer we caught the rain water for washing our hair and for the laundry. We had a big square cement cistern in our basement that was full by the fall but by April that water was all used up. Mondays were always laundry days, Tuesday ironing and so on.

So after many trips with the buckets of snow into the boiler full of melted snow all that was necessary now was that the water be heated to full boiling point ready to be put into the hand wringer washer. To speed up the process Mum took out the two rings of the stovetop so that the flames would be closer and the process wouldn't take as long. That also meant stoking the stove with coal and wood to keep it doing its job. Mother decided to bake a big batch of bread while the stove was going at its full capacity and the oven would be nice and hot. The kitchen was filled with the bread's tantalizing aroma.

I was playing at the chalkboard – we had a framed piece of dark green (about 4ft. square) oilcloth on the wall beside the kitchen cupboard. I loved to scribble and draw on that but after an hour or so I chose to play with something else. I picked up a set of embroidery hoops that were in the living room and sat down beside the cozy kitchen stove and rolled the hoops back and forth between my hands.

Just at one of those times when I was, head down, thank God, rolling the hoops, Mum pulled the boiler of hot water over toward the edge of the stove to put in more wood. Splash! Some of the near boiling water went over me. I screamed, went out of my head with the pain. I ran all around the front room until they finally caught me and removed my heavy winter sweaters and underwear. Those articles of clothing had really kept the heat in so the burns were very severe according to the doctor's later diagnosis - right to the bone in the middle of my back. Much of my skin on my back came off with the clothes. The water was not quite at the boiling temperature – the medical people told me if it had been boiling it would have had air bubbles in it and wouldn't have burned so severely.

Even now at 79 years of age, I remember that day as if it were yesterday. What a terrible shock for my dear Mother! How she nursed me through that whole ordeal! Roads at that time of the year were impassable so Dad had to drive the Overlander down the railway tracks the 17 miles to Rosetown. That railroad had been cleared out for the train returning the Saturday before.

When we arrived at the hospital I was admitted immediately. The Doctor and nurses covered all the burns with Ozonol. To this day whenever I smell Ozonol memories flood back of that hospital stay. To make matters worse I also came down with chicken pox that day so out to the isolation ward I was sent. The isolation unit was a separate little house back of the hospital. But best of all – since we were quarantined, Mother was allowed to be my nurse for the whole time.

After a week it was discovered that the burns were so deep it would be necessary to cautorize certain spots on my centre back. Because of the burns, I had to lie on my stomach most of the time. In those days bed rest was the cure for everything. My stay grew to six weeks and because I had lain on my back for so long I had to learn to walk all over again.

I still have the scars from that splash because in those days there was no plastic surgery or special bandages and medical improvements that have evolved over the years. But I have so many wonderful memories of my Mother's devotion and loving care during those weeks. The Muirland United Church's Ladies Aid sent in a lovely parcel which included a beautifully illustrated Cinderella book. Mother read that to me every night with as many different versions as you could ever think of. I can still taste those delicious oranges and cookies that came in that parcel. I can also remember the special times when Dad came to visit once a week and Mum smuggled him in overnight!

 What a joyous day it was when we returned home to the hazy green and gold of a May morning – a meadowlark warbling its welcome, Gladys and Francis there with hugs, and Ginn ready for a cuddle!

It was doctor's orders that I not go to school for a whole year because my wounds were so very tender we could not risk the chance of them getting bumped. However, my dear Mother would not let that stop me from learning to read. She had been my first class nurse – so why couldn't she be my first class teacher? That she was. By the time I entered school in August, 1931 my teacher, Mr. Clover (with whom I still correspond – he must be in his 90's) tested me and put me right into Grade 2! Mr. Clover was a tall, blonde young man with piercing blue eyes that looked right through you. He did his utmost to teach us but it must have seemed an impossible task with so many students and grades all in one room.

For the first year my brother, Francis, was still in school so we went to school together.

This is Muirland school which I attended to the end of my Grade eleven, taking Grades nine, ten, and eleven by correspondence, with, if the teacher had the time and energy, some help after school. The teacher marked our assignments.

On the preceding page is a 1931 picture – my first year at school. I'm the one in the front row, far right and my new friend, Katherine Mac Millan, is beside me. In the back row, far right is Eldon Woolliams, and beside him is my brother, Francis. Ben MacLeod is in the second row from the back, second from the left in the white shirt. Ben and my brother Bernard were the same age and the best of pals. When I chatted with him just last month on my visit to Sask. tears rolled down his cheeks as he told how they shared their lunches at school and always played together. Ben is now 85. Another friend about whom you'll hear later is Frank Russell - the farthest left in the back row.

I loved going to school, especially recess, for there I made many new friends, with my best chum being Katherine McMillan who was in Grade 1. We became lifelong friends and now in 2003 we live just a ten minute drive from each other and phone or email almost every day. We, with our husbands, even went on an eastern Mediterranean cruise together in 1992. We often say how our life styles have changed over the course of 70 years!

School picture taken in 1935 - I must have been in Grade 7. Take special notice of Katherine, Frank Russell, and Don McIntyre as their names will reappear later in my story. Next to the left of me with the dark tam is Barbara Douglas who lived just a half mile south of the school. We used to exchange week-end visits back and forth in each other's homes. I remember Barbara and her brother Hughie had a Monopoly game which I enjoyed so much I borrowed it for a week and copied it, hand printed all the cards and had lots of fun making the board so that we had our own game. In those days if you couldn't afford to buy something you made it, and had lots of fun doing that.

Katherine

Katherine had a head of naturally curly, fiery red hair in ringlets that tossed around with a flourish when she came galloping into the schoolyard. Most often she did come at the horse's top speed. I wore ringlets until my burn experience but after that Mother just left my hair be its natural very straight self. Even though I secretly envied Katherine her curls I was not sorry to be through with that routine of having my hair done up in those rags most nights.

I had no problem with my Grade two Reading because Mother had taught me well. I loved Art but we didn't have that half as often as I would have liked. Other subjects I picked up on because I listened to the older grades as they were being taught. I understood all the basics of Arithmetic because Mum had covered that with me also and given me lots of "drills" as they called them in those days.

But one day there appeared on the upper right hand corner of the blackboard (I can see those facts just as clearly and vividly in my memory today as they were that morning) – ten questions with missing addends - e.g. $6+?= 11$ or $9-?=4$. Now to those type of facts I had never been introduced. Mr. Clover was too busy with the older classes to explain. The older students (who listened to us read and taught us when they were free) were all busy with their own studies.

What was I to do? I burst into tears. Mr. Clover noticed me and said "Agnes, whatever is the matter?"

I replied, "Oooh, I don't feel well!"

"Would you like to go home?

"Oh, yes please!" I replied.

"Well then, Francis, you'd better take your little sister home."

Now that meant getting the horse out of the barn, gathering me into the cart and taking me the 3½ miles home and then Francis driving the 3½ miles back to school to finish out his day. He would have to miss recess which was his favourite part of the whole day. Consequently he "chewed me out" all the way home, for he knew my illness was not legitimate.

When I arrived home they didn't believe my story either, but immediately shuffled me off to my bed UPSTAIRS and pretended to be phoning the Dr. George in Harris. The telephone was right at the bottom of the stairs so I could hear Mother's side of the conversation from my bed! In those days long distance phone calls were made only in the case of dire emergency and the doctor was not consulted unless you were near death or surgery.

I was terrified, and soon regained my health and confessed to Mother about those awful Arithmetic questions. Mother's immediate tutoring was forthcoming. Next morning I was back in school ready to tackle those Math. questions with no trouble.

Mr. Clover was an excellent teacher who stayed in our community for four years. In 1990 I attended a Muirland School homecoming. At that time a book about the history of our school was compiled. I have included portions of a descriptive account by Mr.Clover which was included in the book. It will give you a clear idea of school life at that time.

History of Muirland School and District by J. W. Clover

The 30's truly tested the moral fibre and fortitude of the early pioneers of Muirland District.

Grades 1 - 12. Eldon Woolliams was the Grade 12 student - quite an illustrious one who later became the shadow Solicitor-General of the Opposition Conservatives in the Federal Government (from Bow River, Alberta) and Calgary where he practised law.

Perhaps I was sort of the "anchor" teacher of the early 30's. I initiated various ways of trying to keep all grades working at the same times and the blackboards were full at all times for seat work. Never enough board space, so often used prepared seatwork issued handwritten on paper. Combining grades, eg. 4,5 and 6, would encourage students to learn faster in some grades and subjects. I had one blackboard on pulleys that would pull up over the lower one and usually used for seatwork for Social Studies. The teaching end of the classroom had a raised platform or dais, which I always thought I would like removed.

Materials were scarce. Chalk was about the only material I ever dared to order. I used kerosene (which I provided) on a cloth to keep the blackboards clean and the chalk dust in control.

I initiated on my own a very, very constant writing away for Health posters, Health material, Science material, mining material eg. "The Story of Asbestos", "The Story of Lead, Zinc and other Minerals", and "The Story of Coffee". It was surprising to find how much interesting material was available from writing to various major companies who were interested in supplying material. It was good advertising on their part and no cost to the school. Posters would brighten up the walls of the school. There were Health charts the pupils could fill out on their own daily - Did I clean my teeth, wash my hands and face, comb my hair, etc. Gold, silver or coloured stars were the awards, or a pencil, eraser, scribbler, awarded by the teacher.

The teacher had to do the janitor work, fires, repairs, etc. for the same yearly pay which was $450 or $500 when I left. I was always dressed in tie, suit, and neatly pressed pants and shiny shoes.

Church collection was 25 cents tops. Dances - 25 cents which included lunch with some of the best chocolate cake this side of heaven. The Claytons, Russells and Stewarts usually helped with the music.

The desks were mounted on bases with screws in order to keep them in line or to move easier to sweep around. The desks were taken out for dances, etc. There was an attic above the ceiling reached by entering a door above the front porch. It was a real effort to get seats etc. up or down. There was a well which I drained by pulling up bucket after bucket to keep the water from being stagnant. There were two entrance doors, the porch had 2 cloakrooms for boys and girls.

The coal bin was at the back of the school; stove was pot-bellied. The coal bin had at least 3 feet of coal dust. I dug through all the coal dust and picked out all the small pieces of coal - made a shelf to put them on and used them to start the fire and when hot the fine coal dust went on and I burnt up every bit of that coal dust which lasted a whole winter.

The school children were the McLeods (Mac, Bennie, Katie), Palmers (Francis, Agnes), the young Calvert boys, the Russells, the Busbys, McIntyres, Douglas's (Barbara and Hughie), McMillans, Carstairs, Frerichs, Robsons, Eldon Woolliams, Billy Gould for my last year. Apologies for any I have not mentioned.

The Palmers introduced me to the game of table tennis - Mrs. Palmer and Gladys were real pros and taught me all they knew. Mrs. Palmer always said that on Sundays after one had finished all their church duties the rest of the day was for enjoyment and she certainly lived a very very long and abundant life - let's render up a short prayer for all those hardy pioneers.

I boarded at the Woolliams' family for approximately half of my tenure and the other half at Bob and Laura Gould's in their new home near the school. This was much more convenient and I could work up to dark at the school and be home in no time at all. For the princely sum of $25 a month, room and board. It was higher at Woolliams but also much farther to travel.

Transportation in the winter - A lot of the farmers built their little box on a set of runners, bobsled or sleigh runners; there was a little window at the back and a small opening at front to see where one was going. Bumpy but more comfortable that an open cutter or sleigh.

I had a 1928 Model A, a real car for any occasion. In snow, mud, rain, hail or sleet, it never let me down - a true car of the 30's and 40's. The 30's were dry and many were the dust storms. I can remember one special day at school when the classroom was so dark - the dust was filtering through all the cracks in the windows and after the storm there was about ¼ inch of dust on the window sills. It was in the air and when you can feel it gritty on your teeth you know what a dust storm is like. But a true pioneer loves his farm and soil so much that when he comes in from work, his wife will say "Aren't you going to wash your hands before you eat?" He will reply, "It's only clean dirt."

So all the graduates of my classes have gone out into the world and made names for themselves and have become good citizens. There was little opportunity for jobs in my day and many became teachers. All three in my family became teachers; the McLeod family had three and Agnes for the Palmers. Many more would have liked to become teachers but finances stood in the way.

Out of those little white schoolhouses have emerged the citizens of future generations with more resourcefulness than the product of modern schools with all their modern conveniences and computers, etc.

I feel that some of the buildings in the area could be heritage buildings. The McLeod home still seems to be in good repair. I always think of the poet who wrote, "I want to live in a house by the side of the road, and be a friend to man." That could apply to any old time home in the Muirland area.

by J. W. Clover (teacher at Muirland from January 1, 1931 to June 30, 1935)

This wonderful missive has explained so well what a teacher's life was like in our Muirland community at that time. On May 31, 2003, as I began copying and typing Mr. Clover's manuscript into my story I decided to give him a surprise phone call as we did visit him in Coquitlam, BC three years ago.

As I dialled the telephone number I wondered " How will I find my teacher of so long ago? Will he remember me? I always receive a precious card and letter from him at Christmas time, but at his age things can happen. He was born Oct. 16, 1910 so that means he is 92 years of age. I hope he is still in good health mentally and physically."

After two short rings came the crisp clear "Hello."

"Hello, Mr. Clover?" I could never call him

"Jack" - that would seem disrespectful even though we are both very senior citizens.

"Yes?"

'This is Agnes Palmer now Weicker"

" Oh, what a nice surprise! And how are you?"

So the conversation took off and turned into a treasured chat like none one could ever imagine.

What a special dialogue we had! Ninety-two years of age, but his voice is as clear as ever, his mind sharper than ever, and he has such an interest in life. When he told me his age he said "but I still haven't matched your Mother, have I? She was 96 when she died."

He too is planning to write a novel – a tribute to the pioneers of our country. He said it will be called "Down to Earth – the Salt Thereof". I told him I couldn't, at this point in time, come up with anything that poetic for my autobiography's title.

Just as a point of interest below is a copy of the note he wrote inside our 2002 Christmas card. It illustrates, among many things, his wonderful sense of humour.

Dear Agnes & John,
     Thou art so Artistic, dear Agnes, the best student in the old Muirland School. From Grade I to Grade 6 in 4½ years or Jan 1, 1931 – June 30, 1935. Wonderful people in the Marriot area. Rosetown, the hub of the bread basket of Saskatchewan. Nature never lets us down but Weather or Climate is the evil doer and hardship is the result. Gladys is still my No. I reporter, the best speaker at the Cairn reception. She would have been a good newspaper editor. I just finished her Xmas card and now I am writing to her famous sister who is now an artist of great promise in water colours. Amen to that.

Many good wishes
for a wonderful
holiday season.

     Time is a healer but also a terminator in the true sense of the word. We all march to its tune because Time decides our fate in life. This is not a sermon but a fact of life. So like you we should accomplish all our aims and hopes in life so that we are ready to meet the grim reaper, Father Time. This is the best autumn we've ever had but the worst for the Resorts like Whistler. Perhaps the storekeepers will get a little more of that money that would have been spent on the slopes. When are we going to get a crossing to Vancouver Island – P.E.I. has its bridge. Ferries are subject to weather, excessive costs, and strikes. Planes are too expensive as well. The solution is a huge tunnel or a huge bridge to one of the small islands and another to hook up to the big island.
     There's nothing fruitful in this message, but Hey!! Santa is in trouble too with no snow. Have his Elves drop all the gifts from airplanes and avoid the rooftops and chimneys. Lots of love and Auld Lang Syne is near. "Jack Clover"

62

But I must continue my story.

I always loved painting in my spare time – this is a card I made in 1935.

When Francis left school it meant that I was on my own getting there, so Mum & Dad went shopping many miles to the north for a reliable horse for me to take to school.

Benny & I – 1931

The result of their hunt was "Benny" who was very trustworthy, in that he would never run away. But he would never RUN period. He never would go above a very slow trot and that was only after much persuasion by me with a willow switch that was in my cart at all times. The first month Mother rode with me until we passed the first corner one- half mile from home, at the "top of the road" as we called it. "Why?" you might ask.

Well the truth was that Benny would then be a half mile from home and before he would turn the corner he would decide to turn around and go back home. My skinny arms did not have the muscle to pull the reins and force him to go on. So Mother would get him pointed in the right direction for the remaining 3 miles to be covered, and then she would walk home.

However, if I happened to be at that corner just after the Calvert kids had gone by in their buggy with an oat sheaf hanging out the back (for their horse's school lunch) old Benny would see that and just tear along that road as fast as he could trot (never gallop) in the hope of having a nibble on that sheaf as we followed behind. Oh yes, he was a wise old fellow. He could also be very cantankerous when he wanted his own way.

Again I refer you to my childhood diary. Notice the entry for January 20, 1936, in which I state that *Benny ran away this morning and Francis caught him over at the store.*

Perhaps he wanted to be ready to pay his respects on the death of our monarch as you will notice further in that day's entry I wrote *King George (V) passed silently away in the evening.*

One other afternoon in early May the creeks were filling, the robins were chirping their nesting calls, the prairie wolf willows were getting their silvery sheen. The sloughs were puddles of deep, clear, fresh water that looked very tempting to an old horse wending his way home after a day of standing in the school barn. So thinks Benny " Why not wade out into the middle of McLeod's slough that is right beside the road? Never mind the fact that the cart is hitched on to me and little Agnes is sitting in the cart!"

Pulling on those reins as hard as I could and screaming at the top of my lungs had no effect on Benny but a human Ben – Ben McLeod, who lived about a quarter of a mile away heard my yelling, ran down the hill and waded knee-deep out into the water. He held on to the horse's bit and halter and guided us back on to the road. As I have said before – Ben McLeod was 5 years older than me. To this day he still teases me about how he rescued me that day.

Another time there was a cloudburst – rain so heavy as it can only pour on the prairies along with a strong north wind. Buckets of rain were driving straight at us - I had graduated to riding horseback by this time. We were heading north – going home after school about 4:30pm. Benny decided that rain was just too strong coming straight for our faces so turned right around   facing south and refused to go any further until the rain stopped. He knew those heavy rainstorms never last very long. We were a half hour late getting home that afternoon.

One of life's greatest lessons I learned those years with Benny was humiliation. In those days at school one's horse was one's "status symbol". I can still feel the sting when the kids used to yell as I drove into the schoolyard "Hey, Agnes, that's quite a horse you've got there – you'd better tie a knot in his tail or he'll go through the collar!"

one of my prairie sketches

To add insult to injury , Katherine would come galloping up on her beautiful "Lady." In the photo is "Lady" - always with a sparkle in her eye and full of vim and vinegar ready to gallop away at the first moment of suggestion.

Above is my horse, Benny,with my Saskatoon friend, Gladys Dobson, and one of her city friends and me on his back- much to his disgust as you can see by his expression!! That day he decided, in spite of every kind of persuasion, he was not, with all that weight on his back, going to move.

One day when school was out Katherine and I (seven years old at this time) decided to trade horses and very leisurely, because Ben set the pace, ride home from school together. The plan was that I would ride Lady as far as her place – 3 miles west of the school, and then get on my Benny and ride the 4 miles north and east to my place. We didn't take into account that this would mean that I arrived home at least 3 hours later than the time my parents expected me.

After 3 hours of retracing my usual route, checking creeks and ditches, for the memory of Bernard's drowning was always there, Mum & Dad found no clues as to my whereabouts.

The strain was getting to Mother. She burst into tears. Gladys and Francis also began to cry.

Dad said, "I'm going to do some phoning."

Dad phoned the teacher, Mr. Clover, at his boarding place, the Woolliams's.

"Hello, Jack. I'm phoning to see if you have any idea when Agnes left school and where she might have gone. We're getting very anxious."

"Charlie, I can understand your anxiety. But as far as I know she left school in her usual way heading straight for home. But she and Katherine MacMillan are always together – have you phoned the MacMillans?"

"We tried that, and their phone is out of order at the moment, but I'm going to drive over there right now."

You can guess the rest of the story. When they got to the "top of the road" they could see me just ambling along over the Marriott railway crossing, not a worry in the world. But when I arrived home and saw the look on my parents' faces I knew I was in trouble!

But they were so glad to see me they just hugged and hugged me. I knew that I had been very inconsiderate and would never do that again.

Mother baked my favourite cake – her renowned "Jelly Roll". In my memory I can see her yet – carefully removing this freshly baked cake from the warm pan, transferring it to a cloth sprinkled with icing sugar, spreading jam on it, then rolling it into such a picturesque cake. Makes me want to try making one of my own today! On the next page is Mother's Jelly Roll recipe as I copied it out in 1947.

Jelly Roll Cake (Mother's)
3 eggs (beaten separately)
1 cup sugar . Pinch of salt
2 tbsp. sweet milk
2 tsp. B. Powder
1 cup flour
Lemon or vanilla flavoring
Beat egg yolks with sugar & milk.
Beat whites to a stiff froth, then
mix thoroughly with yolks & sugar
Mix flour & b. powder & add to other ingredients
Flavor & bake immed. in mod. oven

Here's the May 10th, 2003 version of Mum's Jelly Roll cake. I baked it for 12 minutes @ 375 degrees. Guess what we're having for tea this afternoon!

Thinking back to my school experiences there is one other occasion that I recall – it was my birthday in that same year 1931, when I noticed a beautiful fluffy yellow, black and orange creepy crawly caterpillar moving along beside the wooden runner that my desk was attached to. It was so interesting the way it would go in another direction if I put my pencil on its head but if I lay my pencil flat on the runner the caterpillar would crawl right over it. Deep in thought and fascination with this creature, I suddenly realized that someone was standing over me. I looked up - Mr. Clover!

"Well! What have we here?? A new playmate for Agnes! If that's the case you can just take Mr. Caterpillar outside for the day and you, Agnes, can stand out there for the rest of the day since you're not working anyway. Stand right by the window so I can see you."

So that was the boring way I spent that birthday. I still think my teacher missed an opportune moment to have a lesson on caterpillars but then the curriculum was very rigid, and after all he did have to tend to eight other grades.

In the background in the previous picture of balky Benny, to the far right is Toby, my next horse that I was allowed to ride to school when I was older and my parents felt I could handle the "speed". Toby would actually break out into a gallop once in a while. Oh! The joy! In May & June, though, Toby had to join the other workhorses and pull the ploughs, disks or seed drills around and around the miles of furrows to be made to prepare or plant the year's crops. Now we are getting into the "dirty 30's" as these years have been well named because of the seven years of crop failures we had plus the economic depression the country was experiencing at that time.

Now when Toby was needed at home it meant that I walked the three and one-half miles to school and back each day. But I found that time just great to experience the wide open prairie spaces, smell the freshness of early morning's clear air, hear the meadow larks and robins singing their romantic songs, and generally sort out my thoughts. Maybe that's why I still enjoy my regular walks. My Mother would think nothing of walking a round trip of 13 miles to have a visit with one of her "girl" friends – Mrs. Bob Carnegie or Mrs. Ellen Pearce who lived east towards Harris. I really think this was a form of escape for Mum from the daily routine of the farm and husband and kids - good for the soul just to chat with another woman. She, too, loved to go for walks well into her 96th year of a very full life.

I mentioned previously that Mother was a midwife (no special training – those pioneer women taught each other) and would, if needed, arrange to be with a friend who was having a baby. Again I refer to my diary, January 12, 1938.

69

It states *Quite stormy tonight. Mrs. Carnegie has a little Baby boy 12 lbs. Mother is down there.*

On the next day's entry it says *Mother still away* and this continues until January 16th when I write *Mother came home today.*

So you see – not only would Mother be there to help with the baby's birth but she would stay and help with the other children until things were getting more or less back to normal. There were six other Carnegie children.

Later when I was taking my Grades 9, 10, and 11 by correspondence, I still attended the one room school and worked on my assignments there so when walking home I would many days be walking, reading, and memorizing poetry as I walked along. No traffic to be concerned about there.

Here we are – an older me (at the front of the row far right, and Katherine is at the head of the next!

After Jack Clover, as teachers I had Harvey Giles, Sybil Woolliams, Pauline Getz, and Amanda Maedel.

Here's Miss Maedel, Katherine and I in front of the school. I was in Grade 11 so it must have been 1939 or 1940.

A card I painted for Mother in 1937 – by this time I was painting my cards and for a bit of spending money, selling them for the exhorbitant price of 10 cents each!

Here (photo taken in 1938) you see my Grade 10 teacher, Pauline Getz. My brother, Francis, dated Pauline for a short while. The second picture was taken in 1940 when she married Jack Chapman.

Class photo taken in 1939 by Miss Getz (I was in Grade 11)

This is the last photo together at Muirland school. From left to right – Donald McIntyre, me, Katherine MacMillan, and Doug Robson. Because we had been together in the same grades at the same school for our 11 year learning journey, we had come to know each other very well and were close friends. We went in to Rosetown High School for our Grade 12.

What an exciting day it was for me, in Grade 11 when I got my first bike! There I am with Katherine and Donnie Mc Intyre in front of our school.

The bike came from Eaton's catologue and arrived at Marriott station. I sold gopher tails and rabbit skins to help pay for that bike.

All the teachers at Muirland were hard working and dedicated but I give the

73

greatest credit to Sybil Woolliams (daughter of Frank & Gertie, our neighbours). Here she is as she taught us in 1938-39.

Here is Sybil (now Mrs. Conley) taken on her 90th birthday – March 14th, 2003

After Sybil left Muirland district I lost track of her for 30 years then tracked down her address. I then wrote her a letter telling her how I appreciated her as a teacher - how she got me going in the right direction with my studies. She said when she received that letter she just sat down and cried with joy, then wrote me a note to see if she could come and visit me in Victoria. She spent Easter 1988 with us. What a special reunion that was!

Sybil Conley (nee Woolliams), Marjorie Smallwood (nee Angell) and I at our home in 1988 when Sybil came to visit. We are all three descendants of three Englishmen who came together to homestead in Canada.

Since then Sybil and I correspond and phone regularly. She lives in Palo Alto, CA. John and I motored down and visited her there in 1995.

Marjorie Smallwood and I became close friends when she spent her last years in Victoria.
At 87 years of age Marjorie passed away on August 14, 1998. Two years previous to that Marjorie presented me with a precious needlepoint picture of a prairie harvest scene- such a wonderful keepsake of a very special friendship! This picture now hangs in my sewing room at 6630 Buena Vista, Victoria, BC.

Recalling Sybil's teaching, even though she had many grades to teach in that one room, and several lessons to prepare and mark, she still took time after school to spend up to an hour with her Grade 9 correspondence course students – Doug Robson, Donald Mc Intyre, and me. She would get us up to the blackboard doing Algebra and Geometry problems, writing out French vocabulary or anything else with which we were having trouble. She marked all our assignments giving such encouraging comments, or if we were getting errors there would be the remark, written with that familiar red pencil, "Ask me", and we would do so after school when the younger children were dismissed for home.
Then came the Christmas concert – the most important event in the school year as far as parents and children were concerned and the success of the teacher was dependent on the calibre of that concert.

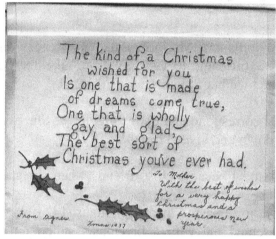

The kind of a Christmas
wished for you
Is one that is made
of dreams come true,
One that is wholly
gay and glad,
The best sort of
Christmas you've ever had.

To Mother
With the best of wishes
for a very happy
Christmas and a
prosperous new
year.

From agnes.   Xmas 1937

How I loved to draw and paint!

My sister, Gladys, explained very clearly in the article that follows all about those special Christmas concerts. She wrote this for the 1990 Muirland reunion book – the same one from which I printed Mr. Clover's account about our school.

As a student who grew up at Muirland School, I remember one of the highlights of our school year was the Christmas Concert.
Early in November the teacher found time to work in practise on a program for the concert.
The whole school would line up on our small stage for "O Canada", carols and other songs. Each child of the school took part in the program according to their age and talents. It seemed we practised our plays, songs and recitations and drills for days.
Costumes were a special part of the concert. The mothers of the students made the costumes.
One of the problems for our teachers was how to keep the children from talking and making noise behind the curtains. Putting on costumes in such small quarters and boys and girls getting to the right side of

the stage to make their entrances all added to the confusion. Behind the curtain was also the prompter, usually the teacher. So many would forget their lines or become stage frightened. Behind the curtain it was difficult for some to keep from giggling and we got in each others' way as we progressed with the concert. Our teacher always stressed quiet behind the curtain. Somehow we all tried to be on our best behaviour.

I can remember my first recitation and my first concert. I had only a few lines to say. When the curtains were opened I got a glimpse of everyone looking only at me. It was an overwhelming experience. I managed to get started on a couple of lines; the people's faces turned into a blur but I finished my lines. I was away for the first time on stage. Behind the curtain I shed a few tears, but it sure felt good afterwards and I never minded talking in front of an audience since.

I remember going the 3 1/2 miles with the team of horses and sleigh. I remember the cold and the creaking of the runners on the snow. It seemed to take a long time to get to school and the excitement of all our practising and getting ready seemed to build up as we neared the school with the lights blazing from the windows and all the cutters and sleighs parked in the yard. The school was filled to the doors but there always seemed enough room for everyone. Once inside, I had never seen so many decorations - bells and garlands crisscrossed the room and wreaths hung in the windows. It was a different world for me. All the children I had been to school with were dressed up in new clothes and hair fixed just so.. Everybody was just standing around being good. There was the Christmas tree all decorated and surrounded with gifts.

After the concert, one of the trustees usually whoever was Master of Ceremonies would announce that Santa Claus was at Zealandia or Dolly Brae Schools. Then we would hear sleigh bells ringing gradually louder until with lots of stamping and "Ho, ho, ho's" Santa Claus was in the hall. He always asked if we were good boys and girls, and we always agreed we were. Santa Claus usually wanted to kiss the teacher if the teacher was female and that was glorious fun for us. Besides the presents that were handed out, they always managed to have a bag of candies with an orange in it for each of us.

After Santa Claus was gone, we could circulate around and be as noisy and have as much fun as we liked until lunch was served. Sandwiches and cake were served from the girls' tiny cloakroom. Coffee was made in a boiler which I think must have come from one of the neighbours close by.

Although cash was very scarce in the 30's Mother always managed to have a really special outfit ready for me for the Christmas concert. Now this is how she engineered such an undertaking – it was quite a long- range project. **First** she planted, nurtured, and harvested two large gardens. **Secondly** she traded the excess garden produce with our nearest neighbour, Mrs. Wilson, for wool from their sheep. **Thirdly**, this wool had to be thoroughly washed, spread out in the sun to dry, then we spent the winter evening carding it, teasing it, and pulling it apart to get all the seeds and tiny bits of grass out. We all helped with this third step. **Fourth step**: Mother bought many yards of bright coloured broadcloth, made lovely machine quilted double bed sized covers filled with that fluffy, cozy pure wool we had prepared. She used her little sewing machine that sat on the kitchen table and had the little wheel on the side that Mother turned by hand. **Fifth step**: she traded these beautiful quilts with Mrs.Angell from Saskatoon for her three grown daughters'clothes that they no longer wanted. **Sixth step**: Mother then made brand new outfits for me, Gladys and herself. That was "recycling" of the 30's!

This is a back view of the type of hand cranked sewing machine that my Mother used in the 30's

So that's how I had my fashion statement for the night of all nights – that Christmas concert! It was my first year at school so I was seven. I remember a turquoise blue velvet dress trimmed with lace that Mother made. I was so proud of it. As we drove to the concert with sleigh and horses I found myself filling with excitement. I entered the school experiencing a sense of great expectation, eager for the moment when the curtain would rise. When I came out on that stage, said my piece and everyone clapped, I thought I was a real Hollywood star. This is what I had to say (with actions):

" When I was a little girl just so high,
Mother took a little stick and made me cry;
Now I'm a big girl Mummy can't do it
So Daddy takes a big stick and hops right to it."

One night we had a masquerade party at the school and Mother dyed cheesecloth to make me a gorgeous costume as an Italian gypsy dancer – bright yellow top, very full bright red skirt. Somewhere somehow Dad acquired a tambourine. I danced my way to first prize that night!

When Sybil was our teacher I was given the part of Miss Canada in a Christmas concert play. I wore Sybil's long green satin dress with silver maple leaves pinned all over the slim straight skirt, as I leaned over the wounded soldier who lay dying on the battlefield. This was the year of the beginning of the second World War so it was on everyone's minds - likely a theme for the entire concert. Sybil wrote the play and had us dramatize it. I loved drama and later studied it at Univ. of Sask. Teachers' summer school. There will be photos of that class later in my story.

Besides putting on the Christmas concert in which we all participated I remember so well that year in June Sybil got us involved in a debate with parents invited as audience and some as judges. The topic was "Be it resolved that our antedeluvian ancestors had a better life that we have today." What a keen debate that was – complete with rebuttals. Certainly excellent public speaking practise – I recited my side many times to the ditches, birds and grasses along the way on my walk home from school. I was on the side of our ancestors – we lost!!

Agnes (age 13) and the close neighbour kids, Elaine & Leona Wilson.   At last I had close neighbours to play with – and by this time Leona and I often played school. You can imagine who was the teacher – me. I knew from then on that when I grew up I wanted to become a teacher. Leona never complained.

My friend Katherine MacMillan – notice the ringlets which were auburn red with beautiful gold highlights. She's obviously all dressed up ready for Church and Sunday School. In these years I used to ride horseback down to the United Church Sunday school and service at Muirland School. I'd be in a dress, even on horseback, for, in those years, Mother and Dad frowned upon the wearing of slacks on Sundays. It was a day of rest and best clothes. If we were to have a big dinner with extra guests on Sunday Mum would try to have the veggies, desserts and most of the preparations made ready on Saturday .

Mother was an excellent cook – especially noted for her desserts and pastries, an English specialty. She made delicious steamed puddings which, when served, would be smothered in a tasty sauce. Probably this is why I have always regarded desserts as my favourite part of any meal (and have been teased about my "sweet tooth") which I don't deny I have.

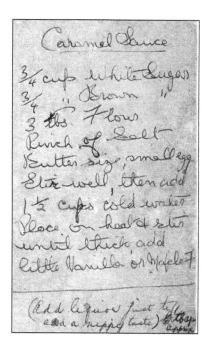

This is Mother's sauce recipe as written in her own handwriting. She dictated the note I added at the bottom. Age has discoloured the paper on which it is written.

When I was 10 years of age my sister Gladys and brother Francis were dating and going to dances which were held almost every Friday night in our Muirland School or neighbouring GlenEagle, or Dolly Brae schools. Gladys seemed to be going steady with a handsome, athletic fellow from Ontario. His name was Alex Franklin, and he had come out the previous fall to help out with the harvest as it was the custom then to bring in extra help from eastern Canada. He was 30 years old and worked for Ernie MacMillan (Katherine's uncle). They got along so well that Alex was kept on for the rest of Ernie's life as a year round hired helper. Alex, an excellent skater, played hockey better than the best of that time. He took Gladys to all the dances even though he danced only the square dances (of which there would be about two per night) but Gladys was a popular girl, and a good dancer so the other fellows kept her feet flying, while Alex chatted with the guys at the back of the hall. Sometimes they slipped outside for a "nip" at a mickey of scotch or guzzled a bottle of beer. Gladys saved all the square dances just for Alex.
In those days the girls all sat at one side of the school and the boys on the other. When the live music started the boys would head over to ask the girls for the dance. Often girls would have two or three dances promised ahead to certain fellows.

Alex drove a Model T Ford. He was very generous and always seemed to have the cash my parents didn't have for extra fun for our whole family. On Saturday nights he would drive up with the Model T - Gladys, Mum, Dad and I would pile into the T and to Rosetown we'd go for the evening. What fun that was for me! We would usually go out for supper to the Chinaman's (the only restaurant in town). Dad

usually gave me 25 cents spending money and I would have the greatest time shopping for something special just for me. Of course it ended up being something for my crafts or school supplies.
When Christmas time arrived Alex had a parcel under the tree for me – and just having a tree was exciting – Alex bought us our first– we could never afford one. Before that Santa always left   the parcels on my little red table in the living room.

When I was ten Alex gave me the loveliest pencil box with tiny drawers full of coloured pencils, crayons, a booklet, eraser, and about four little samples of tempera paint. I thought I had died and gone to heaven!

When I was eleven he gave me a Five Year Diary which I faithfully kept up to date. I presented that diary to my darling grand-daughter, Heidi, when she graduated from Grade twelve. I have borrowed it back to help me recall some of the incidents I want to tell you about.

(sample of inside pages of my 5 yr. Diary)

Mother and Dad and Ginn

On one of our Saturday night trips to town when I was ten years old, Dad and I went to my first movie – "The Count of Monte Cristo." Dad bought a bag of jelly beans on which we munched. I felt very special being there – just Dad and I.

Mother's note on the back of snapshot - *Charlie and I camping two years ago now we don't even run our car& Woolliams's lost theirs through financial circumstances.*

Postcard front

back of above postcard

Pictured above is a postcard sent to me in 1941 (note the stamp) from Mother and Dad when they went on a long awaited camping trip to Waskesui.

Standing in the boat pictured on page 33 with Mother is Fred Scott, our faithful hired man who was with us for many years. Because cash was so scarce in those years I'm sure he must have been working just for the board and room and the company of friends. He was an Englishman who seemed to have no other family but us. He was a small man - a very clean, tidy person who loved children.

Notice the front of our Overlander car. Mum & Dad borrowed our neighbour, Gordon Douglas's tent that summer and away they went on a much deserved camping and fishing trip.

The note on the card reads:

Dear Agnes-
We had a splendid trip here, stayed at "Prials" over the weekend in Saskatoon, went to church Sunday morn was lent a nice hat something like my own. We were going to camp there but they wouldn't hear of it, didn't see Angells.
Love. Mum

The Prialls and Angells were friends of our family. Mother loved hats and she always looked so great in a hat. In those days ladies were not allowed in the Catholic church unless their head was covered with a hat or veil!! (So different now).

According to my recollection my parents only managed to get away on 2 camping trips- this one to Waskesui and one to Lake Meota- in the 18 years I lived at home. They just couldn't afford even the price of gasoline. When they did get away it was a very special holiday just for them. Gladys, Francis and I looked after the house and animals at home.

Mum and her "catch of the day"

Dad and a friend – I'm not sure who the friend is, where or when this was taken but what a happy picture of my Father! One of Dad's hobbies was photography so he very likely developed and printed this in his home dark room.

I never experienced sleeping in a tent until I came to B.C.

Being the youngest of my family I never felt the strain and worries of the 30's as did my parents and older siblings. I do remember when the railway car of food came from Ontario to help out the Sask. families. The apples were super delicious, but the frozen cod fish was hardly edible. Mum tried cooking that fish in every different way she could think of but it still had an unpleasant aroma and tasted and looked like shoe leather. Because of Mother and Dad's ingenuity and good management we kids were never hungry.

One winter, much to my proud Dad's disappointment and shame, we had to go on "Relief" (called **WELFARE** today) just to have money for the basics.

Mother used to sell butter, cream, milk and eggs to Layton Angus, the Marriott store keeper, to help pay for our groceries. This all came to an end when Layton was diagnosed with undulant fever. One of our cows was tracked down as the germs' source so all of our herd had to be slaughtered! No-one in our family developed the disease.

Layton rapidly recovered but that was the end of Mum's wee business and for a few months the end of our own source of milk.

In the 1930's Dad's health was giving him a lot of trouble. Mother nursed Dad through pneumonia and pleurisy many times. One year my father was too sick to farm. He had developed the early stages of tuberculosis – characterized by cough, pallor, and advancing weakness. The doctor ordered complete rest. That meant he spent all that winter upstairs in bed. The alternative was to go to Saskatoon Sanatorium where a lung was collapsed and the patient was laid up for a very long time. We were not allowed
to go close to him – no hugs or kisses – even for Mother, because it was known to be very contagious. This was hard on all of us, and just terrible for dear Dad.

Later in 1944-45 extensive research was being conducted at Rutgers University in New Jersey and at the Mayo Clinic in Minnesota. This research led to the development of streptomycin used in the treatment of various bacterial infections, including TB.

But this discovery did not come in time to help Dad in those years. Mother, Gladys and Francis carried on with the farm work and hired help when needed. Mother didn't only care for the house and family, she stooked, stacked, shovelled grain, poisoned gophers, did chores and raised chickens. Gladys and Francis helped until they were old enough to go out and find a job to earn their living.

When Gladys was 16 years of age and out of school she went out to work as a nanny and housekeeper for Grace Lamarsh at Anglia, SK. Gladys worked there for three months. As so often happened in the 30's, there was no cash to pay help so she was given a cow (delivered free) as payments for her three months' work!

Dad was not too happy about that as all animals had to be fed and hay was scarce because of the drought. Frank Woolliams sold a cow for 29 cents profit after shipping charges were deducted. They had that cheque framed for show later.

To quote Gladys's account *"When the 30's came that was the worst of all. The stock market crashed and down went the farm prices. Eggs 8 cents a dozen, wheat 47 cents a bushel. The land became parched and dry. The air was dusty and dark from the dust storms. Mother and Dad hauled water to the gardens. The grasshoppers came and ate the crops* and gardens. The Russian thistle blew in the yard filling the fences and trees. The army worms arrived in the garden - the worms were on everything and even ate the tops off the onions. They were gone as fast as they came but so was the garden.

Down through the years I can hear Mother's voice with her little quotations. She would never allow shoddy work. "Anything worth doing is worth doing well."

Another favourite quotation of hers was "Never put off for tomorrow what you can do today." That hurried us along for chores and homework.

"A stitch in time saves nine." We learned to sew and mend.

One of Mother's best quotations was "Waste not, want not." That one kept us from wasting many things. We never once doubted Mother's deep love for each of us but if she did not approve of our actions she could stop us with just one firm look from those bright blue eyes.

But hard financial times did not stop romance from flourishing. Young folks still went together for long walks, picnic lunches under the trees, horseback rides to church, cuddled up in the backs of Model T's and Overlanders, or went to the sleigh-riding parties, skating parties, box socials and dances that were the popular events for couples of that time.

There was a "Little Theatre" group in Muirland district. Gladys and Alex belonged to that – Alex played the part of the butler in "The Importance of Being Earnest". Gladys took on another character. She was, from a very young age, very talented in reciting.

Like my brother Francis, she could memorize lengthy poems and passages. It was truly amazing, but Francis could, right up until his death, still recite the passages they had at Christmas concerts of his time. Not only did he know his own part, but he remembered all the other kids' lines because he would listen at rehearsal time, and served as an understudy for all of them if the teacher needed him.

Gladys (now age 21) and Alex (age 31) were spending more and more time together and becoming very fond of one another. So one evening of July 4th, Gladys's birthday, the moon was shining brightly in a starlit sky and this loving couple were sitting   parked out on a private prairie road.

Alex, clasping Gladys's slim, dainty fingers in his big, warm, gentle hands, said, "Gladys, I love you - will you be my wife   sometime in the near future? Right now I haven't the money to buy us a house or farm   but I am trying to gather enough into my bank account that we will be able to build a house and at least rent some land."

Gladys 's hands shook.   Her heart pounded so hard she thought her chest would explode. Tears of joy filled her big blue eyes. She felt so happy and giddy she wanted to sing. After a few moments of thought and hesitation she said,"Yes,Alex, I will marry you some day. I know we will have to wait until our finances are in better shape."

Alex then presented her with a beautifully wrapped tiny box. When she opened it there was a beautiful ring with a sparkling diamond set in shining white gold with a platinum setting.

So the years went on with Alex continuing to court my sister – coming to visit every Wednesday evening and Saturdays and Sundays – in summer driving the Model T from Ernie MacMillan's where he worked (5 miles south). In winter the snow created problems – I can still picture in my memory's eye Gladys and I watching for her lover out the front window, temperature around 40 below zero, snow at least 4 ft. deep, it was around two o'clock on a Sunday afternoon and there the Model T appears at the "top of the road", gets solidly stuck in the   snowy road. Out jumps Alex with the snow shovel, works awhile – we could see the snow flying in all directions- and on he drives. Sometimes it seemed as if he dug out most of that half-mile road get to see his Gladys! When the wind blows on the prairies the drifts get high and hard. That's when we'd see Alex drive the T right over the top of them, but most often he wasn't that lucky and down it would flounder.

In any case he never once missed his bi-weekly visit and you may be sure it was every thing to Gladys. The rest of our family all loved to see him come. He was becoming an important part of our little group. Dad was even getting used to the idea of his precious daughter getting married some day.

In February of 1936 Mother and Gladys had been having some long secret talks in which I was not allowed to share. The two of them had decided that Gladys should go into Rosetown for a medical check-up so an appointment was made for the next Friday afternoon.

Alex decided he would go along. Since the winter roads couldn't be trusted, they decided they would take the train from Marriott.

Right about then one of my back molars decided to get "jumpy."

I said, "One of my back teeth hurts".

Mother and Dad both took a long hard look into my mouth. Dad said, "We'd better get her to the dentist before she develops a toothache."

Gladys, in her ever considerate and generous way, spoke up "She can come with us on Friday."

So we caught the noon train out of Marriott for the half hour trip to Rosetown. We checked into the Rosetown Hotel – one room for Gladys and I, one for Alex.

Gladys took me to the Dentist, got me a 2pm appointment, then went to her Doctor for her check-up.

After my dental work, I walked around the three blocks of town stores gazing in store windows. To me that was exciting. At this point I had never seen any bigger town than Rosetown. When I was twelve Mother and I went to Saskatoon on the train to visit Angells and Dobsons. I was utterly amazed at the wonders of a flush toilet and electric lights and toaster! We never did have electricity on our farm. All my reading, studying and painting was done by coal oil lamp or (once a week) gas lamp. Gladys Dobson had a bicycle and that's when I learned to ride a bike – on paved parking lots and streets it was so easy compared to our rutted or sandy farm roads. After that I really wanted a bike of my own but I had to wait another four years.

Mum crowded as much as possible into my first city experience. One day we started out early in the morning to visit churches. At that time all churches were left open for drop-ins. I was well impressed with all the statues in the Catholic churches – my first view of the inside of one. We took in a supermarket, and library. The only books I had literally "devoured" at school were "The Bobbsey

Twins" and the "Book about Brownies," and a "History of England." Our school library took up one two foot shelf.

Dad had "The Writings of Byron," and "The Stories behind the Operas." I never could get off on them. But Mother's and Gladys's "True Stories" I would smuggle upstairs to read every chance I got! Francis used to get some "Cowboy and Western Stories" that kept me intrigued for awhile but I grew tired of them.

In the evening of our day in Saskatoon Mum and I went to a movie. By this time our feet were swollen and suffering from all the walking we had done so we both discreetly took our shoes off while we watched the film.

Back to my stay in Rosetown – I returned to my hotel room to find Gladys sobbing her heart out! Alex was there with her. They asked me to go to the theatre just a block from the Hotel. They wanted to be alone.

I couldn't imagine what was wrong. I thought it must be connected to Gladys's medical check-up and I was terribly worried. But in those days kids were to be seen and not heard so I just took it as my usual being brushed aside whenever there was "grown-up talk."

My 5yr.Diary entry for that day – February 14, 1936 just says *Go to Rosetown on train with Gladys and Alex. I got a tooth out and a tooth filled at Doctor Fitzpatrick. Went to Shirley Temple show tonight.*

Later Gladys came and tucked into bed alongside me as we were used to sleeping at home. She didn't want me to be scared. I could hear her crying as we tried to settle down to sleep. I was about ready to cry too because it hurt me so to see her so unhappy.

"What's wrong?" I asked.

"Agnes, I'm going to have a baby!"

"Oh", said I. "that will be just the greatest fun for me – I've always wanted a little playmate of my very own."

"Dear, you just don't understand. Alex and I are not married. Wait till we get home and you'll see what Dad says."

I soon went to sleep in a jubilant mood thinking about a baby coming to our house to stay! I couldn't understand why that wouldn't be just the greatest news for everybody.

The rest of our Rosetown visit seemed to be just muffled conversations (in which I was not included) between Alex and Gladys. I was quite relieved when we boarded the train Saturday morning heading for home.

Now in those days discipline was the rule and we lived with strong sexual reserves. Sex was never discussed with children in our home. Maybe because Mother never had a mother of her own to tell her about the "birds and the bees" she herself didn't feel comfortable with that topic. Even when I left home to Saskatoon Normal School I was given no sexual education but I soon gained information necessary for teenage survival from some of my more worldly girl friends.

Sex outside the bonds of marriage was not only frowned upon but often punished, in a subtle way or outright. A quick wedding was often the solution to avoid the gossipy condemnation of the community. Muirland district was no exception. In some cases, teenage girls were sent away from their families and after having given birth, were   persuaded or forced to give their babies up for adoption.

When we arrived home from Rosetown Gladys and Mother immediately went upstairs. I knew they were going to have a serious talk. Down they came to face Dad with the news. Now my father was a very stern, strict man and not always thinking before he spoke.

   When Gladys told him her "news" he just looked at her and said "Well! You've made your bed – now lie on it!"

Very soon Gladys and Alex were married. The Muirland community, as was the custom, put on a dance and wedding shower for the newly married couple. Among the many beautiful gifts of linen, pots and pans and china with which they were presented were several sets of what we later called "depression glass" and which now is a collector's item.

To this day I do not know the exact date of their marriage. The family never did celebrate or acknowledge Gladys and Alex's wedding anniversary until they reached the 50th year and then we did have a gathering with tribute and gifts. By this time my Dad had passed on, but even then Mother was reluctant about having a celebration (didn't attend) – I suppose she was concerned lest the exact date be discussed. It seems so strange but that's how deeply the stigma of a baby's "early arrival" affected that generation.

Olive (Francis's wife) made the anniversary cake. Olive created masterpieces in cakes and all through the years has never failed to have one ready for any special occasion in our family be it birthday, wedding or anniversary.

Gladys and Alex's 50th Wedding Anniversary

From left to right – Agnes, Olive, Jan, Alex, Gladys, Francis and Chuck Franklin (Gladys & Alex's son). Photo taken, April, 1986 in Sask.

Now, once again, let our minds travel back to 1936:

The arrival of this darling fair, curly haired baby was the most wonderful event that could ever have happened for our family!! Gladys and Alex named him after both his grandparents – Charles Benjamin Franklin. He was a great joy to all of us and especially to me for Gladys continued to live with us until Charles (he later became nicknamed Chuck) started school and I went away to Normal School. To me he was and is, to this day more of a brother than nephew. After all, he is only twelve years younger than me and I am ten years younger than his mother.

Notice the patchwork quilt in the photograph on page 43 – made by Mother and Gladys. They used to order bundles of coloured scraps of cotton fabric from a classified ad in the Western Producer. They were not high priced and very useful for quilted projects.

Agnes and Baby Charles

 Please take note of the lovely striped sweater I'm wearing - knitted by my Mother – bright orange and white complete with white collar also hand knitted. Our house is badly in need of a paint job – another by-product of the depression years. Paint was a luxury families could not afford!

Charles Benjamin Franklin.

The writing below the baby on the Model T picture is Gladys's as she wrote on the back of the snapshot.

Here you see Charlie in our yard in the baby walker on which Gladys, Francis, Bernard and I learned to walk. That same walker was brought to BC by Mother & Dad when they moved out. In it Gary and Francis also bounced and bumped their way to walking. In later years baby walkers have been banned as being unsafe.

Another point of interest – in the photo background you can just barely see our "Bennett Buggy" - a common sight in the 1930's. It was a horse drawn cart made out of an abandoned car with rubber tires, the front removed and usually drawn by one or a team of horses.

This brings to mind a very comical story from my childhood.

One frosty Saturday morning in November Alex and Gladys decided to take a trip in to Rosetown for the day. As usual little sister, Agnes, tagged along. Grandma would babysit - delighted to have baby Charles all to herself. Dad gave me my usual 25cents for spending money. We three climbed into the Bennett buggy and snuggled our knees under the blankets to keep us warm. We also had three hot bricks at our feet to keep them warm. Mother had heated them up in the oven prior to our leaving Off we went at a good clip as Alex had chosen the liveliest of the horses to be the team to make the trip.

We spent a fun day in town, going out for lunch at the Chinese restaurant, then browsing and shopping. After all, I did have that special allowance to spend!

After much deliberation I made the big decision to buy a ball of beautiful blue yarn. Mother had taught me how to knit so I was itching to try out my newly discovered craft.

By about 3pm Gladys and Alex were ready to head for home so we piled back into the Bennett "chariot" and off we went at a flying speed. That team of horses were wanting to get home as soon as possible. By now the temperature was down to 30 below zero with the afternoon sun slipping below the horizon.

We felt cozy and warm the three of us tightly fitted into the seating space. We were within a half mile of home taking the short-cut road across the field, horses trotting at their fastest after 16 miles of trek from town, when one of the traces broke. It startled both horses, the shaft hit the snowy ground, the team broke completely away, and the cart was up-ended

The horses headed for home at full gallop. Gladys, Alex were thrown clear. I crawled out from beneath the heavy cart – covered in snow, laughing at our misfortune. Luckily no- one had even a scratch. Our only concern was to gather together all our parcels from the shopping.

Gladys and Alex teased me for years because all I was concerned about was my precious newly purchased yarn.

"Where's my wool? Where's my wool?" I kept saying. It was finally discovered buried beneath a clump of snow.

The other follow up incident of the accident about which Alex teased me was my "brownies" as he called them. These were a pair of <u>brown</u> panties that I was wearing and made their appearance that afternoon as I toppled and crawled out from under the cart. They were fashionably made for me by Mum who sewed <u>all</u> my clothes, and I presume that brown was the only coloured fabric she could locate when the need arose. You can be sure I didn't let any of my school friends see them but it wasn't always easy as you've probably noticed in some of my pictures, girls at that time wore dresses even when riding horses.

Proud Alex with his baby son, Charlie

Charlie and Grandma Palmer

Charlie with the truck his Daddy made for him. The tires were the tire ashtrays that were popular promotion gifts from GoodYear Tire Co. for many years.

We all, including my Dad, loved Charlie with our whole beings. It was such a joy to have this happy little boy in our midst. Now as I look back on my many years of knowing Chuck who became such a wonderful man, devoted to his wife, Jan, daughter Tracey, and her family, and to his parents, I can only say "What a gift from God was that baby presented to us by Gladys and Alex!"

Now as his mother, my dear sister, Gladys (now 89), is contentedly spending her days in the Kyle, SK. RestHome. Chuck (now 67) and Jan faithfully visit her as often as they can and keep track of her special needs. Their telephone calls and visits are the highlights of Gladys's life.

Gladys, Olive and I when I visited my precious sister at Kyle, SK

March, 2003.

Charlie

Charlie and I – that's our barn and granary in the background. The cement form you see in the photo of Charlie is part of a dream that Mother and Dad had of building an addition to our house but there were never enough funds to complete it so Mum planted lovely bright geranium and cosmos beds inside there. There was also inside there a tiny little well all cribbed out ready for the renovation that never came about.

When Charlie was six years old he contracted scarlet fever – a terribly dreaded childhood disease. Gladys and Charlie were still living at home. Our home was quarantined – Alex couldn't even come for his bi-weekly visits, and by this time I was away in Saskatoon at Normal School but couldn't be at home for the spring break holiday – I stayed with Francis & Olive. Little Charlie was several times near death but Mother and Gladys nursed him through the whole ordeal – Mother even used a wee drop of brandy when necessary. Mother and Dad always kept brandy on hand for that medicinal purpose.

One Valentine's Day afternoon in early February, Mother called out to me "Agnes, who is that coming down the road on horseback?"

I went out on the front steps and looked. "Oh no! not Peanuts!"

Sure enough it was Laurie Heal (nicknamed Peanuts) who was at the dance at our school the previous evening. He was about sixteen or seventeen years of age. I was fifteen by this time. Peanuts seemed to be taking special notice of me but I had shyly turned away. I wanted no part of his attention not only because I didn't really like the name "Peanuts" by which everyone called him, but at this stage I had no interest in the boys!

103

Take note of the diary entry for Feb. 14, 1940 – especially " *He is a darn nuisance.*"

FEBRUARY 14

1936 ...

1937. Today is Sunday, St. Valentine's Day, I got a dominion seed house book. On Friday. Alex was up today Mr. and Mrs. Calvert are still in hospital.

1938. I went to school. 30° below. We had a valentine party. Lots of fun. Mr. Calvert drove the Calverts. I got 11 valentines

1939. Went to school. We are going to have our party on Friday, the seventeenth.

1940 Did not go to school today as I have a cold. Ned brought me a Valentine box of Chocolates. He is a darn nuisance.

But what was I to do? Being the bold brave female that I was at that time I said "Mum, I'm going to hide upstairs.   Please tell him I'm not home."

My dear Mum cooperated fully and said what I had asked her to say.

So Peanuts came, left a heart-shaped box of chocolates and went on his way.
I never did see Peanuts again – he lived in a neighbouring district and the last I heard he and his parents had moved away.

My parents and other adults seemed to have a saying in those days. When they talked about me they would say "How old is your daughter?" and when I would say "Sixteen" they would say "Oh, sweet sixteen and never been kissed!" For me that was the truth. But that state of deprivation was soon to change.

One of the boys who lived just a half mile from our school started to wait and watch for me when I would be walking his way on my way home. I was sixteen, almost seventeen by this time and Sid was a couple of years older. He was a handsome, excitingly Spanish looking young man who had such dreamy eyes that could make a young girl swoon.

We would flirtingly chat for a mile or two with Sid asking if he could take me to the next school social and dance. I was thrilled with the invitation and quickly agreed to the idea. A kiss or two were exchanged.

That was my first taste of romance.
I thought I was in love. When I got home I secretly told my sister all about this wonderful boy friend I had acquired.

This all took place when Mother and Dad were on one of their two camping trips I mentioned earlier in my story. On Sunday afternoon, further to our previous walks during the week, who should arrive for a visit and stayed for supper with us - yes, you've guessed it – Sid! Francis was away for the week-end so that left Gladys and Alex, little Charlie, Sid and I. We had no trouble passing the day.

After supper Gladys and Alex decided to go for a little drive just to look at the crops and take Charles for a spin. They hopped into the Model T and away they went.

Sid and I sat down on the couch and looked at my photo album. Sid's arm slid around me as he was becoming very amorous and was gently persuading me to lie down while he lay there beside me and we continued to chat. Gladys and Alex were not gone very long when they arrived home to find us stretched out in this "comfy" position.

Gladys and Alex looked so shocked I knew they were not happy about something. Gladys just said, "Agnes, get yourself up –that is not the way to entertain a boy!"

Truly I was that naieve – just plain ignorant! Sid left soon after, and Gladys certainly explained to me that night about the anatomy of a man and how easily they could be aroused. At first I couldn't believe how babies came about and that my parents must have carried on such an activity to bring about my being. My dear sister had just given me my first lesson in sexual behaviour!

But that lesson did not detract from the excitement and anticipation of the upcoming Friday night dance at our school and my date with Sid.
On Thursday night I went to bed with curlers in my hair and could hardly get a good hour's straight stretch of sleep those rollers were so uncomfortable. Oh! the price of vanity!

When Friday evening rolled around Gladys fixed me all up, put make-up on as only Gladys could do so well to make me look my sparkly best. I was a skinny flat-chested specimen at this stage of my growth. I planned to wear my favourite red sweater and a navy skirt I loved that Mother had made. My dear sister decided that I needed a little padding where my breasts should have been so she took two of Dad's white pressed handkerchiefs, tucked one on each side in my bra. Boy! did I ever feel shapely.

The only problem was that later as the evening of dancing went on, the handkerchiefs slipped put of place, and the necessary "bumps" appeared one at the side and one at the back! The necessitated a quick trip to the cloakroom to put everything back in its right place.

But that was not my only problem. As the evening progressed Sid seemed to have forgotten all about me and had turned all his attention to a new girl who was visiting from Zealandia. So I went home with Gladys and Alex – broken hearted and full of tears.

Later that night in bed Gladys put her arms around me and consoled me. "There are lots of other boys out there that you'll meet who will be even nicer than Sid. Just wait and see!"

I soon recovered.

 I was now perhaps at my most radiant and budding bloom of youth, happy, bright, and full of life and love.

When June of my Grade eleven correspondence year arrived we three students (Donald, Douglas and I) from Muirland were required to write departmental exams in Rosetown.   All through our high school Donald and I were very keen competitors regarding our subject marks. It was a wonderful incentive to study. Our final results would be very close if not exactly the same.

Going in to Rosetown and staying with a strange family – I remember I slept on a hide-a-bed in their living room, got up early, did a little last minute cramming, then walked three blocks over to this "big" (four classrooms) school. It seemed big to me with my limited experience. I was nervous. We had to wait a month for our exam results but oh! the joy and relief that July day when I rode my bike over to the Marriott store to get the mail and there was that special envelope. I frantically tore it open. I had top marks in everything .

As my diary entry for July 30, 1940 says

I got my results in the mail today. I have passed into Grade XII. Average 81.6%

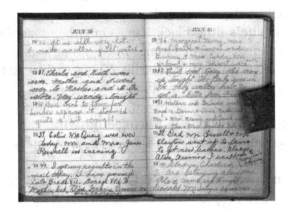

On June 19, 1940 there was another very exciting event in the Palmer family. My dear brother Francis married Olive Nash in the Catholic church in Biggar, Sask. Olive was the oldest of eight girls born to John and Della Nash. Her uncle and aunt, Ira and Ella Nash, had six boys.

Francis and Olive Palmer with attendants Veronica (Olive's sister) and Lawrence Massey who married a year after on March 21, 1941.

John and Della Nash were Irish Catholic. John would hitch up the team and sleigh in the winter or horse and buggy in the summer and faithfully drive the necessary miles to make certain that the family got to Mass on Sundays. On Friday nights he took the older girls to the nearest dance but John was not that caring as to whether the girls got away to school. The dances offered the best opportunity for his daughters to meet the eligible young men of the community. John believed that marriage was the best route to financial security. The Nash girls were all very pretty and soon were caught up in romances.

Olive, being the oldest began to wonder at the regular arrival of new babies in their household. This year when we were reminiscing about our childhoods Olive told me she really believed until she was well on in her teen years, that the babies came in the doctor's or midwife's little black bag. Only then was she told the truth by one of the neighbour girls. At that time, most young women entered marriage completely ignorant about sex and childbirth. Young girls who had lived like nuns were suddenly plunged into a courting ritual.

Olive was a beautiful bride who was a wonderful wife and mother to their very special daughter Vina whom I'll tell you about in later chapters.

Although Olive had not been able to go very far in her school grades she is one of the most talented, creative people I have ever known. As my brother, her beloved husband once said to me, "Olive can do <u>anything</u> you ask her to!" and that is true.

(one of my recent paintings)

108

Francis and Olive's wedding cake

To my utter disappointment I was writing my Grade eleven exams the day they were wed so I did not get to attend any of the ceremony or celebration but my husband, Johnny, and I were certainly present for their 50th anniversary in 1990. (Johnny passed away just four months later).

The same wedding foursome 50 years later.

The bride, Olive, wears the same gown 50 years later! My dear friend, Winnie, and Gladys seated on the right.

Olive and her seven sisters and two sisters-in-law – Gladys on Olive's right and me on her left.

My husband, Johnny Graf, dancing with the bride, Olive, in June 1990 in Rosetown, SK.

Then came 1940 and Grade twelve. At first Mother and Dad thought they would send me to the Rosetown R.C. Convent (a residential school) but decided they could not afford the tuition costs. They, along with Katherine's parents, decided that it would be a good idea for Katherine and I to stay together in Rosetown and do "light housekeeping" as they called it in those days. Katherine would be taking her Grade eleven.

This proved to be a good idea – both Katherine and I, being strong, healthy girls, survived very well. On Fridays we would go home for the week-end. Our Mums would send us off well stocked with food that would last us for Monday and Tuesday. Wednesday and Thursday we would survive with bologna sandwiches and cornflakes, Friday we would be home again. Cooking was not a priority in our lives.

Rosetown High School where I took my Grade twelve

Katherine and Mrs Cooke on the steps of the Cooke residence where we stayed in 1940-41 when I took my Grade twelve. A very kind landlady, Mrs. Cooke rented out two rooms.
 The other girls staying there were Viola Taylor and Gladys Macauley.

In the photo we have left to right, me, Gladys, Viola, and Katherine.

My Grade twelve class at Rosetown High School   1940-41
George Munro was Principal. Nellie Briese taught French.

I had certainly learned how to study independently with correspondence courses so when we actually had four fulltime teachers I did exceptional work with ease. Still being the country girl I was serious about my assignments and home work was always on time. My chief competitor here was Eileen Stratte (also a farm girl but two years older than me). She received the Governor General's award that year for the highest average in final exams in the province of Sask. She beat me out by one mark.

The Graduation and Convocation ceremony was held in September. I was already in Saskatoon taking my teacher Training so could not afford to come home to attend but my French prize was mailed to me. Although I could not speak a word of French – no conversational study in French by correspondence – I certainly did know my vocabulary perfectly – hence the prize. Perhaps that's why it is not written in French (as my precious grandaughter, Lindsay, noted when I proudly showed it to her).   I plan to give it to her when she graduates from her Grade 12. She is fluent in the French language (having been in "French immersion" classes all through elementary school). What opportunities kids have nowadays!

GRADE IX

The N. McVicar medal for general proficiency, Hamish Garland; the Dollar Store prize in mathematics, Lawrence Wickett; the W. Richardson prize in English, Lorne McConnell; the Unique Theatre prize in language, Ruby Brown.

GRADE X

The J. H. Smith medal for general proficiency, Elaine Aseltine; the Dr. C. A. Fitzpatrick prize in languages, Lois Dinwoodie; the A. H. Burton prize in mathematics, Cuthbert Muttitt; the Dr. G. Gordon prize in English, Noreen McIntyre.

GRADE XI

The Dr. J. A. Perrin medal for general proficiency, Gerry Williams; the W. S. Elliott prize in English, Elsie Lypchuk; the B. L. Colwell prize in mathematics, Wilma Ahrens; the A. F. Gledhill prize in science, Morley Aseltine; the Dr. C. M. Lowry prize in languages, Roy Perrin; the Safeway Store prize in history, Eldom Muttitt.

GRADE XII

The C. W. Holmes medal for general proficiency, Eileen Stratte; the Olive Ferguson Memorial medal in English, presented by the S.D.B. Club, Dorothy Wright; the Graham Brothers prize in mathematics, Barbara Hare; the King's Limited prize in science, Betty McLeod; the G. F. Williams prize in French, Agnes Palmer; the Cafe DeLuxe prize in history, Don McIntyre.

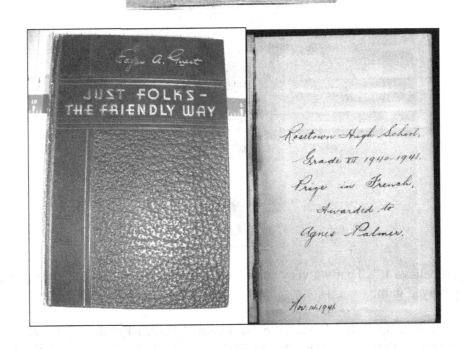

But my life at this time was not all studies. I began to take notice and enjoy the attention being given to me by the boys. In February of 1941   I received, in the mail, a bundle of six valentines – all signed from "Guess Who?" I think Frank Russell knew I would know his handwriting – after all he went to Muirland school a few years earlier.

The next Friday evening Frank phoned to ask me if   I was going to the social evening at Muirland school.

I replied, "Yes, I'll be there, with   Gladys and Alex."
"Great!"said Frank. "I'll see you there!"

When music burst forth and the dancing began there was Frank asking me for the first dance and several others as the evening progressed. Then he asked if he could take me home.   This was an indication that he would like to be my boy friend and I thought that was a pretty good idea.   Frank was a popular young man, good dancer and first class at softball playing which was one of my favourite sports.

So it was as that year went on, it was Frank and I, along with his brother Jack and Olive's sister, Bernadette went to dances at Muirland, and neighbouring schools, Glen Eagle, Dolly Brae and to the halls at Valley Centre or the Marriott Hall which was about five miles west of Marriott siding. We also attended all the school picnics where we usually played softball as Frank was on the Muirland Men's and Katherine and I were on the Ladies' Team. Katherine was the catcher and I was the pitcher. What a lot of good healthy fun we had that summer!

Can you believe it? That's a very suntanned me in my ball cap and resting after a closely played game.

That same year Jack and Bernadette (nicknamed Posie) Frank and I went in the boys' Model A Ford to the Saskatoon Exhibition. Left home early in the morning, had a fantastic day at the fair – we went on every ride, took in all the side shows, ate lots of treats – Frank and Jack had lots of spending money as their farm had a good crop that year. Frank bought me a red, white and blue anchor pin set with rhinestones as a souvenir of the day. After a very long and full day and evening, by the time we drove the seventy-five miles home again it was early morning and the sun was just coming over the horizon. Dad was not pleased. Mother could see what fun I had enjoyed and soon got Dad calmed down so I could fill in all the details of the day.

Frank Russell as photographed at our Saskatoon Exhibition outing, 1941

Frank Russell in front of his parent's home near Harris, SK, 1941 on a sunny August afternoon.

Here is Frank taken that same Sunday

with his two brothers, Jack to the far left and Ken to the far right, with Bill Carnegie, beside Jack, Sid Carnegie (remember that first heart throb!) now in uniform, and home on leave. We are by now beginning to feel the reality of war as the boys who were in our classes at school and who grew up with us are one by one being taken into war duty.

Here I am in one of the dresses Mother created for my going away to school. I included this picture to show you how much loving care Mum put into designing these creations – no quick-sew jobs – but carefully trimmed and beautifully sewn partly by hand and part on her little hand propelled sewing machine.

Then came September of 1941, the day I was to leave my home on the farm and go to school in the city. I'm sure this was the culmination of many months of planning on the part of my parents. Mother had been saving her money from her sales of butter and eggs.

Normal School tuition was $75 per year – a huge sum in those times! Mother had found a boarding place for me sharing a bedroom for $15 per month. She had sewed for many long evenings to send me off with a complete student's wardrobe which included a stylish winter coat all trimmed with Persian lamb fur (recycled from the Angell girls' cast-offs). She bought me (ready made) the prettiest floral housecoat of cotton seersucker wrinkle-free fabric. I loved it - not only because it was the first article I had owned that was not home-made, but it was strikingly pretty and colourful.

When the actual day of leaving came, and my suitcases were loaded in the back of the Overlander, I was experiencing mixed feelings. I was excited about the new world of city and learning I was entering but so sad to say good-bye to Mother and Dad and the farm. I cried for most of the way to Saskatoon. I remember Dad saying "Well! I guess she loves us a little bit anyway."

I knew I probably wouldn't get home again until Christmas at the earliest. In those days long distance phone calls were made only in cases of death or dire emergency. We would write letters but oh, how I would miss Mother and Dad, Gladys and little Charlie. I treasure these photos on the next page taken around that time.

Mum + Dad. August 1940.

My darling sister, Gladys and I

I felt a new chapter in my life was beginning.

Several years later (in 1975) Gladys wrote this **"Psalm for a Sister."**
I am going to include it here because it helps to convey the closeness Gladys and I
have always felt for each other:

I will lift up mine eyes and smile as I give thanks for my sister:

My radiant, complicated sister — who is more than a sister — who is my friend.
(blessed is the woman who has one like her, and thrice blessed if she has more
than one).

I will give thanks to the good Lord that we were children together, sharing the
same room and for years the same bed.
I am grateful for the memory of her small body warm against mine.

I rejoice to remember our play-houses and paper dolls and plans. Our secrets
and surprises, even our quarrels.

I feel a deep and poignant longing for those days when we were girls together,
life-hungry, love hungry, each fighting our own battle, yet supporting each
other against the world.

My sister, oh Lord, my beautiful sister often maddening, always understanding,
always fun.

Thank you for this woman who shared my parents, my past, my blood, who sees
my whole - the beginning long ago, and the person I am now.

My sister, whose faults are so clear to me — and dear to me, just as my faults
are to her. Yet for all our differences, and the miles that lie between us, we
would still battle for each other.

I laugh for the joy of my sister, all the comedy, the gaiety, and I sometimes
weep for my sister.

I long to comfort her, to hold her close as we held each other for comfort and courage as little girls.

Dear God, please take good care of her, this sister I love so much.

Teacher Training and first four years teaching

1941 - 1946

Now I'm in the big city!

Being 17 years of age, I just made it under the required date – one had to reach the magic age of 18 before you would be allowed to graduate as a teacher.

I found Saskatoon to be such a busy, bustling place but loved every part of it. My landlady, Mrs. Wheeler, was a chubby, motherly widow who had two daughters, Toots and Frances, three sons overseas in the war which was raging in Europe at this time and Jerry at home. Her ten year old son, Jerry, was home from school more that he attended, because he was suffering the after-effects of rheumatic fever. I shared my small bedroom with the daughter Toots who was my age and worked in a grocery store in the Mayfair area. We slept in the same bed, shared the same clothes cupboard, but got along just fine for the ten months I stayed in their home.

Frances & fiancé Doug   Toots and Doug   Mrs.Wheeler

I rode my bike to Normal School. Classes were not held in the Saskatoon Normal School building because that was taken over by the RCAF for training headquarters. Our teacher training (called Normal School) was conducted at

123

Wilson School. Mr. Seeley, the Principal, always spoke nostalgically about "that beautiful building on Avenue A" when he was feeling misplaced by the military.

 When I enrolled and registered we were asked to state our religion. I filled in RC although I had never been taught any catechism or attended a Mass. At that time any RC teachers, before they graduated, were expected to receive a certificate in Catechetics and thereby go out into a community well prepared.

Consequently Kay Philion, Secretary of the Normal School, a staunch, devout Roman Catholic, called a meeting after school the second Monday of the term for all the RC students. I went to the meeting, learned that I was completely lacking in the background necessary to pursue the catechetics programme. I stayed back after everyone left the gathering.

 I said, "Miss Philion, may I please have a word with you?"

"Why yes, Agnes, how can I help you?"

I explained my predicament to Miss Philion.

"Why that's no problem - I'll phone the sisters at Rosary Hall – a Sisters' Monastery downtown, and we'll get you started on some instructions."

Next day she came to my classroom and motioned for me to come and talk to her. She had it all arranged for me to attend private classes every Saturday morning.

So then began my weekly bike ride or walk (when the winter snows came) for an hour of inspiring religious teaching by the dearest little nun, Sister Lucy, with prayers to learn and some home study, plus regular attendance at Mass in the St.Paul's Cathedral downtown. This, hopefully, would culminate in my receiving my first Holy Communion and Confirmation.

In the spring the Sisters invited me to stay over Friday night at Rosary Hall where I had my own private room which gave me space to meditate and pray. The Communion and Confirmation took place on Saturday morning in the Cathedral - just for me and two other teenage candidates. The Bishop was celebrant.

That whole ceremony and week-end was very special to me. I appreciated the privacy of it all as in those days I was really quite shy with strangers. Mother and Dad couldn't come in all that way from the farm.

Miss Philion was there along with my little teaching Sister Lucy and several other nuns from Rosary Hall. In those days the nuns always wore their habits. This gave such a reverent background to a special breakfast held for us first communicants after the service in Rosary Hall with gifts of lovely little holy cards with handwritten inscriptions from several of the Sisters and a beautiful ceramic crucifix from Miss Philion.

Miss Philion (now in her 90's) and I in 1991 at Miss Philion's home on 2nd Ave. in downtown Saskatoon, SK

John and I attended my Saskatoon Normal School Reunion in July of 1991. Miss Philion, because of age and infirmity, could not attend the banquet and other festivities. So I phoned her and we arranged to visit her in her home.

She was delighted to see me again after 49 years! She remembered all about our past friendship and was happy to hear of the joy that my RC faith has been to me and how, through my church I have made so many wonderful friends, not to mention the fact that I have been blessed by two very special marriages – both husbands being Roman Catholic.

Her home, a beautiful bungalow built in the 1920's, with a small garden, was surrounded by high rising office and apartment buildings. But she said she refused to give in to the realtors' generous offers – she would stay there as long as she could. A real feisty old lady – had taught special education in USA for several years before retiring. Now her only companion was a big old cat.

It meant a lot to me to see Miss Philion again and I know it was a treasured moment for her to be remembered by a student of so many years previous.

I also had the privilege of renewing acquaintance with my Normal School Physical Education (we called it PT – Physical Training) teacher – Miss Dorothy Leard, who was now Mrs. Jackson.

Miss Leard in 1941.

Here I am with my PE teacher of 50 years previous.

Because we were in the midst of WW II our PT in those years included a lot of marching and very regimented exercise. We had to be ever ready to be called into service if needed. Even our Saturday afternoons were to be spent marching. Miss Leard would be at the parade ground leading us.

This was not my favourite pastime and I skipped out as many times as I could get away with. That's why you don't see me in this newspaper clipping of the best. I was absent that day – probably riding my bike along the Saskatchewan river trails. My inborn love of the wide open spaces was with me then as it has been all my life.

But as I look at this clipping I recognize many of my classmates and so feel a bit guilty that I was not there that day marching for my country.

A Smart Platoon From Normal School

The pick of seven platoons of girls at the Saskatoon Normal School taking drill, first aid and other training designed to fit them for useful service in a war zone, line up after a detailed inspection by Lt.-Col. R. W. MacMillan, officer commanding, 2nd Battalion, S.L.I. Colonel MacMillan said the precision drill of the girls was "exceptionally good." The students are under direction of Company Sgt. Major Mary Knight of the S.A.T.S., and R.S.M. N. Unger. The training given these girls is considered by Principal C. P. Seeley of the Normal School as part of their curriculum, which they will put to good use when they begin teaching in Saskatchewan schools within the next few months.

The boys were not excepted from this activity – many of my classmates are in this picture. No co-ed groups - might have been more beckoning to attend if there had been!

2nd Battalion Trained These Normal School Cadets

—Photo by Hollywood.

THE 2nd Battalion, S.L.I. (Reserve), its ranks depleted by enlistments in the Canadian Army (Active) is starting an intensive 10-day drive for recruits. It has to have them and privates, non-coms and officers are going to do their best to have the gaps in the ranks filled. Each man in the battalion will try to get another man to join up.

The 2nd Battalion is doing another job that but few Saskatonians know about. Here are shown Normal School cadets that have been instructed by Sergeant-Major Hazel (inset), who has a dawn to dusk job as instructor for numerous groups who want to know "what's it all about" if it does happen here.

Primary Education was the class I most enjoyed. Miss Irwin was the one who instilled in me a desire and the knowledge to teach the younger grades. She was not at the reunion so I could not tell her so. I will always remember her. Her handy ideas guided me through many years of teaching primary classes.

Miss Irwin

Miss Leard & Miss Irwin in 1941

The other teachers were also memorable. Because it was wartime they had to make many adjustments. We all grieved with our Social Studies teacher, Mr. Cowie, when his son was killed overseas. News of tragedies like this were coming in every day. But oh! the joy when soldiers, sailors and airmen would be home on leave!

My landlady, Mrs. Wheeler, with her three soldier sons home on leave.

Toots and I on the steps of the Wheeler home. Jerry Wheeler with their beautiful spaniel.

Mrs. Wheeler on the same steps.

FranWheeler married Doug that year but the marriage had to be kept secret or Fran would automatically lose her position as married women weren't allowed to work in her company's office.

As this year in Saskatoon rolled by I made many new friends.

Anne Scobie I immediately befriended because she was from Rosetown and her brother Colin had been in my Grade 12 class. Anne and I hadn't met before because she was a year older than me and had been away from home for a year studying music.

One early morning later in September we had a real cloudburst of a rain but I decided the streets were dry enough I would still be able to ride my bike to school. 33rd Street, the route I always took, looked just fine. However looks can be deceiving where prairie roads are concerned. I headed right into the worst gumbo of clay which jammed up my bike wheels. They wouldn't even turn!

As I struggled trying to poke the mud out with a stick, then carrying my bike for a short distance, I looked around and there was another SNS student having the same problem! We both had a good laugh about our predicament, introduced ourselves and became good friends from then on. Her name was Gladys Paul and she was a farm girl from Macdowall, SK.

Gladys Paul and I with the bikes that brought us together.

Gladys Paul from Macdowell, SK

Gladys, Anne and I became great friends and spent a lot of our free time together in that year. Both Gladys and Anne were very musically talented. We all three loved to dance so even put on some skits, songs, and a dance for the SNS assembly programmes.

One of our dance groups - #3 is Agnes and #6 is Gladys. Anne is playing the piano so probably took the picture.

For one musical number we sang and danced to the tune "Oh, Johnny!" I cringe to think of it now, but we had a lot of fun doing it and so we did our part when it was our room's turn to provide entertainment for the whole SNS assembly of 300 or more students!

As you can see I was losing that "shyness" I talked about earlier. All part of the teacher training process!

Agnes, Anne Scobie, and Gladys Paul in 1941. Our nicknames were Palm, Mac & Paulie. Mac came from Anne's second name – Mac Intyre.

Gladys and I visited back and forth in the evenings because we lived only eight blocks apart. Gladys was boarding with her aunt and uncle who went to the Mormon & Latter Day Saints church. Just out of curiosity I went to some of their church services and youth group meetings. I also went to some of United Church services with Anne. With these I was familiar as I had for years at home been riding horseback down to Muirland United church – even received a prize one year for perfect attendance! But even with all this "shopping around" I still felt that the RC church was the one for me so was happy now – thanks to my parents, Miss Philion and Sister Lucy - I was a full fledged member.

Gladys, Anne and I always spent our Sunday afternoons together with other SNS students. Our classrooms were mostly filled with girls because of the war which had taken the strong, healthy fellows into the military. Those who were left were either too young (some, like me, were 17 and, unless you lied about your age, as did Gary and Francis' father you had to be 18 for enlistment) or had poor health, eyesight, or bad feet , or were Conscientious Objectors. All eligible young men (18 to 25) were away in the military training or in the active forces overseas.

Sunday afternoon with friends. Note the coat Mother made for me trimmed with real Persian lamb fur from the Angell girls' cast-offs - they bought the best of designer clothes!

Gladys and Anne with more friends from SNS days.

In those days, when we went to dances girls danced with each other. The few men who happened to be there were in great demand - especially those home on leave - so handsome and mature looking in their smart uniforms.

Our SNS softball team – Anne is 2nd from left in the back row. I'm 2nd from the left in the front row.

My Muirland friend, Frank, occasionally drove in from Marriott to take me to a show. When Thanksgiving long week-end came around he and his Dad arrived that Friday with their farm pick-up truck What a delightful surprise! It meant I could go home with them and see my family. I had so much to tell them about my first six weeks away from home.

Somehow it didn't seem so bad leaving them all this time. I had found Mother and Dad in good health. Gladys and Alex and little Charlie were making plans to build their own home on a nearby quarter of land, so exciting things were happening.

By the middle of October Mr. Seeley, our SNS Principal, called together ten of the students who were showing the best teaching potential. These people, because of a severe shortage of qualified teachers, would have the opportunity to be granted a temporary teaching certificate, to go out to distant schools and immediately begin teaching . I was one of the chosen ten. What a temptation! To start earning especially when I knew the money situation was very tight for my parents.

But the agreement was that after finishing the teaching term one was to return to SNS the next September and complete the required teacher certification. I had to consider this delayed commitment along with the fact that I was only 17, thoroughly enjoying my year in the city, Mrs. Wheeler was counting on my being with her for the whole ten months, the schools were in very remote northern Saskatchewan, and we had to make a decision that very day. All these factors made me decide to finish my year as planned. My mind was made up. I didn't even phone my parents for advice. It proved to be a wise decision. My older classmates who went had some harrowing experiences.

Christmas vacation time rolled around and I boarded the train for a wonderful two weeks' holiday at home. Little Charles seemed to have grown into a little boy – no longer a baby!

When Christmas day arrived Mother and Gladys had prepared the usual Christmas dinner with all the trimmings. Alex always bought the turkey. As in all English homes in the festive season, besides the Christmas pudding with that sauce (the recipe of which I have previously included), there was always Christmas cake and mince pies or tarts.

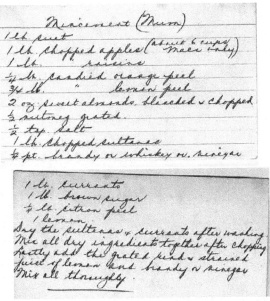

Here you have Mother's recipe as I copied it in 1947. I have used it every year and it never fails - always a big hit with my bridge friends and others.

Even when money was the most scarce in the "hungry 30's" Mum always seemed to find enough funds to buy the ingredients for the Christmas cakes, puddings, and mincemeat. Just sold more milk, butter, cream and eggs or garden produce.

Mother's Mincemeat recipe

That Christmas of 1941 Frank gave me a beautiful gold Bulova wrist watch. He noticed that I had never owned a watch. I was so happy with this lovely gift. He also announced that he planned to join the RCAF in the new year.

Back to school I went early in January. Dad & Mum took me out west, in the Overlander, the 5 miles to the highway where we flagged the bus.

Near Vanscoy our bus got stuck. After the driver and a big strong passenger shovelled and the rest of us pushed we got on our way again. As you can see I still took time out to snap a picture. All part of the adventure!

But by 1942 WWII had caused Canada many losses – some of our own community's sons.

As these young men left home, then graduated in their own fields of training and headed overseas, we knew that we might never see them again.

Awarded Their Pilot's Wings

← Donald McIntyre

PICTURED here is a group of Saskatchewan lads who successfully completed their service flying training at No. 15 S.F.T.S. at Claresholm, Alberta, and have been awarded their pilot's wings. Front row, left to right: J. P. Coggins, Saskatoon; J. A. Barrey, North Battleford, who has a brother in the army overseas and a brother in the Canadian navy; V. D. Ball of Saskatoon. Back row, left to right: M. Thomas, Saskatoon; D. J. McIntyre, Rosetown; A. C. Smeed, Regina; J. M. Dalgleish, Melfort.

Notice there is Donald McIntyre (my chief competitor in Muirland School) now receiving his Captain's wings. I felt so proud of him!

These airmen from Saskatchewan graduated recently from No. 1 Wireless School, Montreal, as wireless operators ground, wireless mechanics, or radio telephone operators. Front, left to right: A.C.'s E. Martinson, Battleford; A. E. McGrath, 640 18th Ave. N.W., Calgary; A.W. M. F. Brealy, 3924 Dewdney Avenue, Regina; A.C.'s C. W. Phillips, Outlook; L. A. G. Harris, 714 Seventh Avenue, north, Saskatoon. Middle, left to right: K. R. Dowson, Mossbank; M. Malic, Ridgedale; P. Soruski, Candiac; C. F. Chapman, Estevan; C. E. Linnell, Glenworth. Back, left to right: G. G. Graham, Rosetown; H. A. Cullen, Kelliher; N. S. Dingwall, Asquith; F. F. Stang, Macklin; A. H. Woolsey, Penzance; and B. D. Duer, Bradwell.

Back row, extreme left is Garfield Graham who was in my Grade 12 class in Rosetown.

Gary and Francis's father, my first husband, Johnny Graf, also enlisted in the Canadian army in 1942. As I have mentioned previously, although he was only 17, he said he was 18 which was the required age to enlist. On the next page is the only picture I have of Johnny in uniform.

Johnny and his Mother in 1942

John Weicker, in 1942 when he had just enlisted in the Canadian army. He will appear later in my life when I become Mrs. John Weicker.

On February 9, 1942 another wonderful, blessed event took place in our family when my precious niece, Vina was born.

Olivia & Unxia – aged 3 wks

I didn't get to see her until my Easter holidays – what a wee bundle of love!

Frank – 1942

Easter holidays, 1942 - the next time Frank came to visit he was in uniform.

My parents were becoming concerned the friendship between Frank and me might be getting serious. Mother always encouraged me, as far as the boys were concerned, to "love'em all a little" - a favourite expression of the time.

Now she said, "Agnes, we know Frank is a good boy, but he is going away to war. He will be travelling all over the world, meeting lots of nice, pretty girls. They will all fuss over him and chase him as many women do because the men do look so smart in their uniforms. We would like you to finish your teacher training and teach for at least a few years."

"Yes, Mother, I understand what you are telling me. I am not ready to settle down yet. Frank is a wonderful friend, has always been so good to me, and we do have a good time together, but we have never talked of marriage as yet. I agree it is time to call this romance quits."

So that week, when Frank, along with his brother Jack and Posy, came to take me to the dance at Marriott hall, I told him that I would not be going with him. He wasn't too broken hearted because he just drove on - right over to Nash's (2 miles away) and took Levina, another of Olive and Posy's sisters, to the party.

He probably, like me, felt it was time for a change in routine. Levina and I were good friends for years after and often laughed about that evening.

I returned the beautiful gold watch – should never have accepted such an expensive gift in the first place – and Frank's Mother became its proud owner.

Mind you, when Frank returned in July after his graduation with his Pilot's wings shining forth on his uniform chest I wondered if I had made a mistake. He did look so handsome – made any 18 yr. old girl's heart go a flutter! We did continue to correspond and his letters were so interesting as he described the wonders of flying.

The SNS graduation party (now you call them proms) was a gala affair in a downtown hotel. I was determined to attend, invited Harry Pearce, a good friend from home, and borrowed my sister-in-law, Olive's, wedding dress for the occasion.

Then I was home for the summer, reading the ads, then writing out applications for my first teaching job! There were two ads that interested me. One was for a Catholic teacher in Gravelbourg, in southern SK. The other was for Polar Crescent School near Asquith – just 25 miles west of Saskatoon.

Both phoned saying I could have the job if I wanted it. I chose Polar Crescent for two reasons. First, it was close to Saskatoon, the city I had grown to love. Secondly, relatives of my friend, Katherine, also McMillans, lived near Asquith. I had been to their home and they were such friendly folks I felt I would know at least one family when I arrived there.

So when the middle of August came Mother and Dad, in the Overlander, took me to my new location. What excitement for me going to my first teaching position!

THIS airwoman and airmen graduated lately at the R.C.A.F.'s No. 1 Wireless School, Montreal, in the biggest graduation ceremony, comprising three classes, yet held there. In the front row, left to right, are E. A. Hogue, Gravelbourg, wireless operator ground; Airwoman 2nd Class C. M. Cronin, Saskatoon, wireless operator ground, and A. Pysden, Foam Lake, radio telegraph operator. Back row: W. J. Lemeke, Wolseley, and C. B. Scobie, Rosetown, wireless operators ground, and R. J. Coffey, Bender, wireless mechanic. —R.C.A.F. Photo.

In this RCAF graduating class is Anne's brother Colin Scobie who was in my Grade 12 class in Rosetown. More reason to clap our hands with pride!

My friend, Gladys Paul, began her teaching at Deer Park School near Prince Albert, and Anne Scobie's first school was in southern Saskatchewan. It was there she received the terribly sad news of the death of her oldest brother overseas, as announced on the Saskatoon Star Pheonix in the clipping on the next page. Gladys and I grieved for our dear friend's loss. Although we were now scattered in our new teaching assignments we kept in touch.

Died for His Country

P.O. L. W. SCOBIE

est son of Mr. and Mrs. ...iam Scobie of Rosetown, ... October 11 in England ... result of wounds received ... action. He joined the ...AF. in 1941 as an observ- ...and was later promoted ...pilot officer, going over- ...s in the spring of 1942, ...ere he was attached to the ...A.F. Word was received by ... parents that he had been ...ngerously wounded in ac- ...ion on October 10, and he ...died the following day. A mil- itary funeral was held at Darlington Cemetery, Dur- ham County, England.

The young aviator was 22 years of age, and was born and educated in Rosetown. After leaving school, he took special courses in electric welding and allied subjects, and until the time of his en- listment had been engaged in his father's machine shop.

Besides his parents, he is survived by two sisters, Anne, teaching in the south of the Province, and Constance at home; and two brothers, Colin and David, both at home.

Pilot Officer P. Finnerty Has Pleasant Experiences

YOUNG ROSETOWN AIRMAN IS COMMISSIONED, MARRIED AND DECORATED ALL IN SPACE OF FEW WEEKS; RECEIVES D.F.M.

ROSETOWN. — The past few weeks have been notable ones for P.O. Patrick Finnerty, young Rosetown airman, for he received his commission, was married, and was awarded the Distinguished Flying Medal, all within a short period.

Pilot Officer Finnerty is the son of Mr. and Mrs. P. Finnerty of Rosetown and he was born in this town 20 years ago. After graduating from high school he enlisted in the R.C.A.F. in June, 1941, and went overseas in May, 1942.

After receiving his commission while on operational flying, he married Joan Dawson of Thurmas-

ton, Leicester, England. The following day he received the Distinguished Flying Medal for outstanding work on operations while previously a non-commissioned officer. Pilot Officer Finnerty has been flying Lancaster bombers. He is now on instructional duty in Britain.

While a student in Rosetown, Pat Finnerty was prominent in field sports and in the Boy Scout troop. His father is a veteran of both the Boer and the First Great War, and is serving in this one with the Veterans' Guard of Canada.

Pilot Officer Finnerty recently received a rubber dinghy for use with his aircraft, from Eileen Auckland of Hornsey, England, and thereby hangs a story of one of the many tragedies of the war.

Miss Auckland was engaged to an airman who flew with the same squadron as Pilot Officer Finnerty, until he was reported "missing, believed killed." When Miss Auckland received the news she decided to use the money saved for her trousseau, to purchase a rubber dinghy, a device that has saved so many airmen from a watery grave. The dinghy was sent to her late betrothed's old squadron, and Pilot Officer Finnerty received it.

P.O. PAT FINNERTY

145

Pat Finnerty was also in my Grade 12 class at Rosetown High School. So every month seemed to bring news of the boys from home – sometimes making us full of pride for their accomplishments, and other times bringing us to tears for the loss of another of our young heroes.

My Muirland teacher, Miss Amanda Maedel married Stan Dunster on February 21, 1942. This is the picture she sent me – we corresponded for a few years after she and I left the Muirland district.

Anne Scobie and I spent a week-end at Macdowell with Gladys and her wonderful family. Here they are in 1942 –Gladys' sister Agnes, older brother Donald, younger brother Leland, and parents Alex and Hulda Paul. We returned there again after we had been teaching when Donald was home on leave from the military looking very mature and handsome in his uniform. Mrs. Paul was of Icelandic origin, also a teacher. We became very close friends. Hulda went back to teaching in her 50's, after Alex died and her family were away. We used to exchange Christmas concert ideas, corresponding regularly, and she came to stay with us when I lived in Kelowna in the 50's. She was a very special lady. Gladys now lives in Ontario but has spent two winters in BC right here in Sidney and Brentwood so we got in lots of visiting, and I have spent some holidays with them in Scarborough and out at their cabin at the lake. We always keep in touch once or twice a year by phone or letter. Gladys is another of my very much loved and special friends and whenever we get together we always have such a good time.

My teacher Pauline Getz and I also kept up regular letter writing. She became Mrs. Jack Chapman in July of 1941 and sent me this photo. What a doll she was!

As you can see, life went on – though we at home were far away from the horrors that were taking place in Europe we kept in touch as best we could – writing letters, knitting socks and other apparel, sending parcels and buying war bonds with any cash folks could gather together. More and more of our men were needed overseas and as the years went by not only the young single boys, but the young married men were being called to serve.

Francis and his grain elevator at Marriott.

My brother Francis, now a grain buyer for United Grain Growers at Marriott, SK, married and a new father of Vina, was called up but because of poor eyesight was not accepted into the military. He was disappointed but you can rest assured that Olive was relieved to have him home again and the U.G.G. were happy to have him in their Marriott branch.

It was the young men and women overseas who were making the supreme sacrifice. Forbes Robertson (whose photo is on the next page) lived next door to Mrs. Wheeler's where I lived in Saskatoon. We all shared the Roberton's grief over this terrible loss of their dear son.

Died for His Country

SGT. FORBES ROBERTSON

23-year-old son of Mr. and Mrs. William Robertson, 605 Thirty-third Street, west, who was killed on air operations in North Africa on April 29. Sergeant Robertson, a wireless air gunner, was flying with a medium bomber group of the United States Air Force and in a letter received here by his parents a few days ago mentioned that he had taken part in a couple of raids lately. "We have our first ribbon of this war up," he wrote, "the American Campaign Ribbon for this theatre of war. It has a brown background with our colors in the centre and Jerry and Italian colors on either side." He had arrived in North Africa in January of this year and was there attached to the American air force. He had previously been attached to the R.A.F. in Britain where he arrived in October, 1941. Sergeant Robertson enlisted on December 20, 1940. He was born in Saskatoon February 2, 1920, and received his education at Mayfair School and Bedford Road Collegiate. He was employed at Clark Brothers and Company when he enlisted. He played hockey with the Mayfair club and was a member of Mayfair United Church. A brother, George, lives at 404 Taylor Street west, and another brother, W. D. at Cornwall, Ont. A sister, Mrs. J. Eaton, lives at 816 Thirty-third Street, west, and another sister, Mrs. A. W. Edie, in the Asquith district.

My Muirland friend, Frank Russell (Now Captain W. F. Russell) of the R., C. A. F. continued to write letters. Frank was stationed in England. He was flying somewhere over there but all letters were censored so he could never tell me much about his missions. He did describe the scenes below – *"houses look like little boxes."*

That soldier boy, John Weicker, at Camp Vernon in 1942.
But I didn't know him then!

But I was young and, even though war was on, my life was not all sadness.

It was 1942 and I was in Polar Crescent School District all set for my first teaching position. I was naturally nervous, this being my first job but I felt I was well prepared because I had just purchased a brand new set of World Book Encyclopaedia. A keen saleslady had talked me into that during my last month at Normal School, the idea being that no matter how skimpy the library would be at my school all the resource material I would need would be between the covers of those fifteen volumes of World Book. I fell for the idea and agreed to pay for them by a sum of ten dollars to be taken off my cheque at the end of each month. So that was my first purchase out of my salary which was to be $700 per annum.

6 of my P. C. pupils Sept./42.

Polar Crescent School, near Asquith, SK

Teaching was a great joy for me. I loved it so very much. I just couldn't believe that I was getting paid for having so much fun. I worked hard but it was very rewarding. My students were Gertrude, Tyra and Harold Mortensen, George Musgrove, Lorena (Dot) Cattell, Mary McNab, Gladys Ewen, Jack and Les Cattell. I have kept in touch with the Cattells over all of the past 60 years. They have become my other " family" as you will discover as my story continues.

Leaving for school with Tony.

When I arrived at Kay and George Chambers, my boarding place 5 miles north of Asquith, I was introduced to Tony, my pony, with the cart which would be my means of transportation for the 3 miles to and from Polar Crescent School. Because I was a farm girl they felt I would have no problem with Tony, a Shetland pony, who had lots of energy but a nervous disposition. They warned me that he hated bicycles. If you happened to meet a bike on the road he would just go wild and balky. I never did meet a bike when he was pulling my cart. He behaved himself just fine for two years. My Grade 7 boys would have him all ready hitched up for me after school. I would jump in the cart. He would take off at top speed. After my experience with "Benny" I thought this was just great.

Likewise in the morning George Chambers would have him all ready for me. But on the morning of April 26, 1944 (my 20th birthday) in Kay and George's driveway, Tony leaped forward in his usual way, but one trace broke. He bolted, throwing me right clear out of the cart, running away and smashing everything to pieces. I wasn't hurt, but that was the end of that cart. No one ever drove him again. We laughed about that for years. It must have been quite a sight!

Agnes Dec 13, 1942.

Kay and George were the dearest couple who welcomed me into their home and set me up with a lovely big upstairs bedroom with a window seat looking south onto the main road. That's the upstairs window you see in the picture. They really pampered me with love and caring.

Kay and George had a dairy farm so would be up early in the morning to set the milking machines. Then the milk had to be cooled in big tanks ready for the milk truck that arrived at 10 am to take the milk into Saskatoon. The Cattell family also had a dairy farm. That was the main industry of that community at that time.

Kay & George Chambers

I had many lovely pictures of my beloved friends, Kay and George, but they both passed away several years ago and I put all their photos in a special album and presented it to their son Larry who lives in Lloydminster, SK. I always chat with their daughter, Linda Kadler when I return to Rosetown. She has a lovely Ladies' Dress Shop there on Main Street called "Lasting Looks by Linda." Larry and Linda had not arrived on the scene yet when I stayed with Kay and George.

Kay and George took part in all the softball games, dances, skating parties, theatre clubs and social activities that went on in their community so through them I soon made many friends. Cattells invited me to their home almost every week-end. Their daughter Winnie and I immediately became good friends. Winnie worked as seamstress in the StyleBest Store in Saskatoon and came home to Asquith on the week-ends. In that Cattell home there were four generations - Winnie's grandmother who lived to the ripe old age of 104, Winnie's parents, and Winnie's brother George and his wife Dora, and their five children. Their daughter, Joanne was born after I left Asquith. What a wonderful family! Quite a houseful but they still had room for me every week-end. Thanks to the Chambers and Cattell families I have many beautiful memories of those two years in Polar Crescent district

My first field trip with my students to Saskatoon. Because there were only 7 (Mortensens were not allowed to go) we could all bundle into Ed Fielden's car for the trip.

Mr. & Mrs. Cattell   Winnie's parents

Winnie - November, 1942.

My first photo of my dear friend Winnie. This treasured friendship continued for 59 years until cancer took her life in 2001. We spent many precious holidays in each other's homes over those years. I had the privilege of being with Winnie through the last week of her life. I was very honoured to be asked by her nieces and nephews to give the eulogy at her funeral. I still miss her a lot, and writing about her brings tears to my eyes and sadness to my heart. But I am ever thankful for the years I had this wonderful friend who knew me so well with all my faults but still tolerated me as her friend. Over the years her family became my family, and she followed with love and devotion all the activities and growth and losses within my family.

Winnie's brother, George and Dora Cattell, parents of my students, Dot, Jack and
Les Cattell

Kay Chambers beside George Cattell's cutter. This had a stove inside – a cozy
means of transportation for the winter months – providing you didn't upset! This
could happen sometimes if you came upon snowdrifts across the road or if the
driver decided to give us a thrilling ride as George Cattell (Winnie's brother)
would do just for a lark. He was such a tease! But it could be dangerous to upset
with the stove going – soon the cutter would be a bundle of blaze which
happened a few times but not when I was there.

Kay, Agnes Dec. 13, 1942.

Kay had preceded me as Polar Crescent's teacher, so was the greatest resource one could ever have to assist a beginning teacher. She helped me organize my first Christmas concert – that important occasion, as I've mentioned before – your teaching career depended on the success of that endeavour.

I received my first parental complaint that December when it was getting close to the concert date deadline. I was beginning to panic as kids were forgetting their lines, or not sure about their stage directions. Consequently I was stealing more and more class time for practising just to make sure that everything would be ship shape for the big night.

That evening the phone rang. It was Mrs. Mortensen.

"Hello! Is that the teacher?"

"Yes, this is Miss Palmer. How can I help you?"

"I just want you to know that I send my kids to school for you to learn them, not to make them into movie stars! You're spending too much time on that concert!"

"Well, Thank you, Mrs. Mortensen, I'll take your advice into consideration."

My first Christmas concert was a howling success thanks to the efforts of Kay (who had lots of creative ideas for the programme numbers) and Dora Cattell and Ethel Musgrove (who were talented piano players) so we had lively accompaniment for the Christmas carols and dances. Of course I have to thank the children most of all – they memorized their lines, never complained about the endless rehearsals, and produced a two hour programme with a V for Victory wartime theme but lots of laughs as well as serious ideas. When you realize that we had only nine students you can imagine the quick costume changes that took place between numbers! My parents came from Marriott to see that first concert. That meant a lot to me. I was so glad it was a success.

Parade of the Toys Drill – Dec. 1942.

Late that night after the concert we drove the 65 miles back to Marriott. Luckily the roads were still open or they wouldn't have been able to drive to Asquith. Winnie came to Marriott for the last week of the winter break and we went back to Asquith on the train. In those years we had January holidays, but started the school year earlier in August so the children didn't have to go to school in the coldest weather.

Winnie & Agnes – January 3/ Heading back to Asquith

I just have to point out my new coat and hat. These were my second purchases (the encyclopaedia was the first) with my first teaching cheque. Oh, what a feeling of independence! That coat was a grey tweed with a red fox collar. The hat was the pill box style of those days – dark green felt with a black ostrich feather. Now how classy is that!!

Gladys + Alex's new home.1

We were all happy that at long last Alex and Gladys would be able to be in
this home of their own! Alex had built it in his limited spare time. It was just a
mile from Mother and Dad's place by road but in the winter we just cut across the
field which was much shorter.

Over the years this little home grew into a pretty little farm settlement with
gardens, barn, garage, and chicken house. Many a wonderful meal we enjoyed in
this Franklin home. When Gary and Francis were growing up we made regular
trips to Saskatchewan and spent many happy times here.

In 1966 Gladys and Alex received a fantastic windfall - a very elderly Ernie Mc
Millan, the man Alex had worked for over the past 30 or more years, died and
willed his entire farm, fully furnished ten room house, and cars, trucks and farm
machinery, to Alex and Gladys. It came as a complete surprise to them. They
had no idea Ernie had stated in his testament (drawn up ten years previous) that
"Alex was as close to being my son as any son could ever be." Gladys and Alex
were always both very good to Ernie and cared for him over his last years. He

had never married so had no children of his own. We were all for happy for our dear Gladys and Alex. No one else could have been more deserving of such good fortune. Here's a glimpse of their new home. We continued to enjoy our prairie visits to this new location.

Another picture of my childhood home on the farm

Once again let your minds travel back to my visit home in 1942 and the changes that were taking place. Gladys and Alex have traded in the Model T for a Model A coupe – now isn't that jazzy?

I have scanned in a page from my "Whoopee" photo album which Kay Chambers gave me for my 1942 birthday. It contains goofy photos and this is a sample. Winnie and I are in the rumble seat of Gladys and Alex's new car.

Moving on to 1943 my friend Katherine McMillan from Muirland, who completed her Grade 12 at Rosetown High School while I was at Normal School, is now in Saskatoon at Business College.

On March 23rd, 1943 I received the postcard on the next page from my sister Gladys. Dad was in Rosetown Hospital at the time.

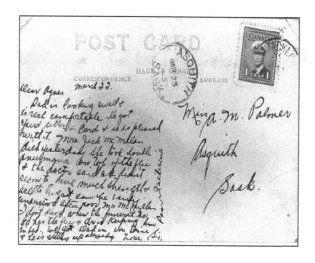

The card reads as follows:

Dear Agnes:
Dad is looking swell and is real comfortable. He got your letter & card & is so pleased with it. Mrs. Jack McMillan died yesterday. She took double pneumonia on top of the flu & the doctor said she didn't seem to have much strength & will to live. It can be easily understood after poor Mr. McMillan. I don't know when the funeral is. Ed has the flu & dr. is keeping him in bed. We got Dad in in time & he is sitting up already.
Love, Sis
Poor Katherine.

Katherine's parents died within two weeks of each other. She was only 18 years old and had her one brother Ed the only member of family left. How sad for my friend. But she was a plucky one. She finished her business course, then headed for Toronto with her girl friends who had connections there.

As you can read, my Dad was also in hospital at that time and had been seriously ill. You can imagine my concern. Both Mother and Gladys wrote to assure me of the improvement in his condition. But in those days telephone calls were expensive – so I was forced to wait for news by mail. You can imagine my relief when I received these cards but I grieved for my friend Katherine. Since I was teaching I did not attend the winter funeral and did not see Katherine for many years until she came out to BC to visit us.

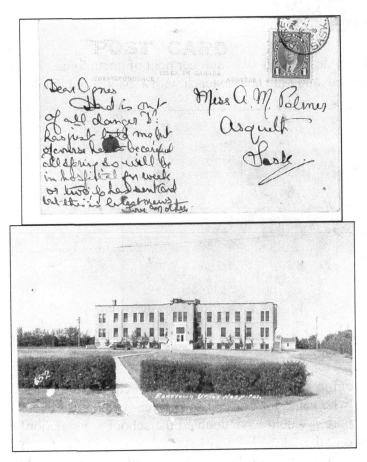

Mother's card reads "*Dear Agnes Dad is out of danger Dr. has just told me but of course has to be careful all spring so will be in hospital for week or two; G. has sent card but this is latest news Love Mother*"

Dad

So once again my dear Dad is over another bout of pneumonia. Needless to say we are all relieved and I am able to teach with a happy and thankful heart.

It was the custom to invite pre-schoolers to the school for parties. This is the adorable group who came for our end of the year celebration in 1943 – if there had been four more it would have doubled the school's population! Only one of them – Faye Cole, the tallest little girl started school in the fall of 1944. The others were still too young and there were no kindergartens in public schools in those days.

I still loved to paint in my spare time. This is a card I made for Mother and Dad
Easter, 1943. The inside of the card is shown below.

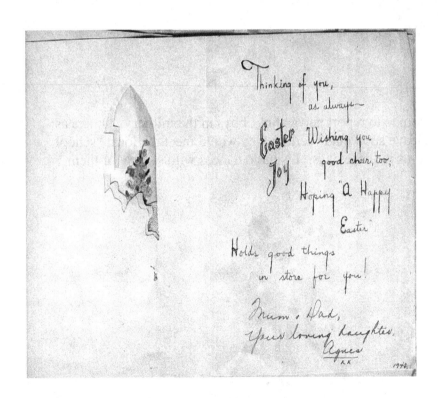

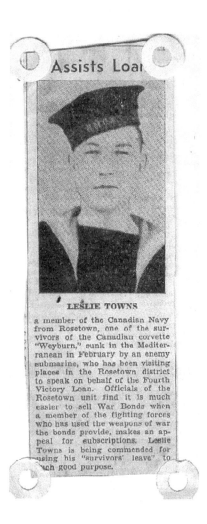

Assists Loan

LESLIE TOWNS

a member of the Canadian Navy from Rosetown, one of the survivors of the Canadian corvette "Weyburn," sunk in the Mediterranean in February by an enemy submarine, who has been visiting places in the Rosetown district to speak on behalf of the Fourth Victory Loan. Officials of the Rosetown unit find it is much easier to sell War Bonds when a member of the fighting forces who has used the weapons of war the bonds provide, makes an appeal for subscriptions. Leslie Towns is being commended for using his "survivors' leave" to such good purpose.

Our newspapers continue to report news of our boys in the military. Others as they came home on leave soon made certain they would meet the local "school marm" as they called us in those days. I went to dances with several of them.

Biking — May, 1943.

Biking was another favourite pastime.

In my story I have included newspaper clippings and pictures to try to give you an idea of what life was like in the years of World War II from 1939 to 1945 - those are my years from the age of 15 to 23. If you can picture how very important these years are for growing up and dating. I was never at a loss for boy friends who would call for me to take me dancing or skating or ball games. I enjoyed their company and for the first year of my life at Polar Crescent I "loved 'em all a little" as Mother had recommended. I remember one week I went to five dances in a row - and still managed to be alert for teaching the next day even though I didn't get home until 1 or 2 am. Those country dances went on until late. But life seemed to be a series of "good-byes" for the liveliest and most attractive men seemed to be home for a short visit and then off to war.

During this first year of teaching I was also studying two University of Sask. correspondence courses – Math. And English, sending in regular assignments . To make our teaching certificate permanent we were required to have six units of credit plus two years satisfactory teaching experience. So this was my first step to attain this goal. That I accomplished. In the summer of 1943 I attended the University of Sask. Summer School, taking a Drama class which I thoroughly enjoyed and achieved top marks.

Miss Helen Stewart – Dramatics 8

Miss Helen Stewart was our beautiful, talented instructress. A pantomime assignment was the one for which I received the most acclaim. I acted out the complete story of "Preparing for a Date" on stage with no props other than a chair and a table. It was great fun. Got lots of laughs, and went over well with the audience of my peers and other University Profs. Below you see the stage on which I performed.

Stage in Convocation Hall. (Summer School 1943)

You can gather that I had lost a lot of that shyness that I mentioned having in my high school days.

Dramatics B · Summer School · July/43.

This is our Drama class of 1943 at the University of Saskatchewan, Saskatoon, SK.

My special friend, Gladys Paul, also took this course and we, along with four other girls, rented a suite on College Drive just across the street from the campus. It was a fun-filled summer.

So now I had my six required credits and with one more year of teaching I would have that important permanent teaching certificate and could move on to other schools or perhaps even farther afield to a different province. This idea was always in the back of my mind.

Our Asquith Ladies Softball team.

That's me at the left end of the back row on page 46. We toured all around, playing in the neighbouring districts in the spring of 1943 and 1944 and had lots of fun, even managed to win a few games.

Skating – November/43.

Skating was another of my favourite sports and took place on outdoor rinks set up around each district. Not always the smoothest surface but a great gathering place on a frosty Sunday afternoon. Can you recognize me in the white jacket? We also went into the arenas in Asquith and Saskatoon where it was much more sophisticated – skating to the skater's waltz or a catchy tune. I'm wearing tube (boy's) skates still from my Muirland days.

But also in 1943 there came into my life a young handsome airman, Donald Mc Nab, whose home was in the Polar Crescent district. His parents had a farm just north of Kay and George Chambers' place where I boarded. He was home on leave and at the Saturday night dance in Asquith. Winnie and I had talked George (her brother) into taking us into town to the dance as we didn't have a date for that one.

Donald soon asked me to dance and we chatted away just to get acquainted as young folks do. What attracted me most about him were his eyes. He had those male eyes that I had never seen before – dark blackish brown. Those eyes made every female hormone inside me start to vibrate and giggle. He told me all about his life in the air force ground crew, asked me about my family and home town, then said "I'd like to take you home." After all it was right on the way to his own place.

That was the beginning of a romance that continued for that leave and any others he had for that next year. Each time when his leave was over, I went with his brother, Glenn, when he took him to the train station. We said good-bye and those wonderful inky dark eyes looked out through the train window as we waved good-bye. We promised to write which we did faithfully – a letter every week. He was stationed in Claresholm, Alta. I loved his letters too. For Christmas he had a professional photo of himself in uniform taken and sent it to me. I treasured this photo and will tell you more about it later in my story.

That same year I had also met another Asquith service man, Angus McTavish, who was home on leave from the Navy. He had been stationed in Esquimalt, BC, but had travelled to Hawaii and other places which to me seemed so exciting and exotic. He was tall dark and handsome, personality plus, and a very smooth dancer. He took me to Saskatoon to the ballroom dances which were very new and exciting to this country girl. Angus was the favourite son of the Polar Crescent district. Everyone loved him and spoke so admiringly of him. He and I also corresponded and for Christmas he also sent me a professional photo of himself in uniform. This photo also had a special place for some time on our piano at home in Marriott.

In March of 1944 my special friend, Frank's parents in Muirland received the all too common telegram – "You son, Captain William Francis Russell, has been reported missing and presumed dead. His plane was shot down over Germany on March 25, 1944."

So now my dear friend, Frank, had been killed overseas. No more of those interesting letters, and another friend gone, never to come back home again. Our whole Muirland community was in grief – Frank was everyone's favourite youth, so wholesome and fun-loving. The day after receiving the fateful telegram, Frank's Mother received a beautiful bouquet of red roses *With Love from your son, Frank* He had wired these roses to his Mum the day before he was killed. How terribly sad for her! Now she had only the memories of her son who would never be coming home again.

This year (2003) when I was visiting out in Sask. and chatting with my old friend Ben McLeod (now 85) he was telling me that he was stationed at the same airbase as Frank in WWII. Ben was also a pilot. He said that he and Frank were sitting talking the evening before Frank went on his last mission. Frank said "Ben, I'm just not cut out for these air raids and bombing activity. I just hate the whole idea."
How many of our young men survived the depression only to lose their life like this in a war which, like all wars, is so hard to understand?

That same spring of 1944 my friend, Angus, was sent home from the navy on medical leave because he had developed a severe case of tuberculosis from spending so much time working in the poorly ventilated lower areas of the ships. He was sent to the Saskatoon Sanatorium, had one lung collapsed and was to spend the next two years confined to bed in that hospital. I visited him every opportunity I had when I was in Saskatoon. Two years is a long time for an active 24 year old man to be confined to a bed but at that time that was the only treatment for TB. He was always so grateful for my visits.

In the meantime I had decided that it was time for me to move on and gain some different teaching experience. Even though I loved Polar Crescent School and all the people in that community, I was restless to see more and meet a new teaching challenge.

Besides all the good-bye parties, I received a proposal of marriage from my friend, Donald Mc Nab, with a gift of a beautiful diamond ring. It was his idea to get married right away – his father had given him a quarter section of the home farm so that he could have a house built on it and start his own farm as soon as the war ended. I accepted the ring, but did not want to get married until the war was over. So we both agreed to wait. Donald drove me home to Marriott that June so that he and my parents could meet. We spent a very happy week there at my home until it was time for him to say good-bye and return to Asquith, then the train to his airbase at Claresholm, AB.

That same summer of 1944 my brother, Francis, invited me to go with him and Olive and his friends Ernie McMillan (for whom my brother-in-law worked) and Layton Angus (the Marriott storekeeper) on a motor trip to Banff and the Calgary stampede. I was overjoyed at the invitation, and one of the reasons they wanted me along was so they could use my liquor and gasoline coupons. These were rationed in wartime.

I also thought that since we would be out in Alberta I might even have an opportunity to slip away for a week-end and go to visit my fiancé, Donald, who was stationed at Claresholm, which was in the vicinity of Banff and Calgary, but when I mentioned this to my family Dad said "Oh, no you don't. I forbid you to go there all by yourself to see him. If you go you don't ever need to come home again. You can phone him and that's all!"

My dear Dad was very strict but it was a strictness born out of deep love and I respected him for it. He could also be very gentle and thoughtful.

We had an adventurous trip. My first sight of the Rockies impressed me immensely and made me all the more determined to make that planned move that was always in the back of my mind. But I would have to start saving up some money because that would be costly.

Olive and I were good company for each other. In Saskatchewan at that time, women were not allowed in the beer parlour, but in Alberta women could go in. So, even though Olive and I didn't drink beer, we were allowed to go in and then the men could sit on that side of the beer parlour which was much quieter and cleaner than the male only side. Francis, Layton, and Ernie were all very fond of beer.

Ernie, me, Olive and Francis in front of the Banff Springs Hotel. We stayed in Cochrane because there wasn't a hotel room available in Calgary – Stampede time.

I did try to phone Donald at Claresholm but had no luck reaching him.

172

Olive took this picture of Ernie, me, Layton, and Francis.

Because we were in the midst of WWII the Calgary Stampede parade of 1944 had

a very military theme .

V for Victory was on everyone's mind.

On the next page you will meet Clare, my English cousin and her husband Roy. I mentioned previously, Clare and I had corresponded ever since I was eleven years old and she continued to send pictures. Clare's parents'home in Southampton was flattened by bombing in WWII with my uncle (Clare's father) succumbing to a severe heart attack. Clare (ten years older than me) married Roy Hayward in 1939. In 1941 she sent the picture of Roy in uniform with their oldest son, Peter. Roy was away for years (in India I believe) and Clare was home in England with three small children. How brave those young mothers were forced to be!

Roy & Peter in 1942

Cousin Clare & Roy in 1940

IT WAS LOVE at first sight for Roy Hayward when he spotted his wife-to-be at work — although Clare Barlow didn't share his feelings.

The couple, both 72, from Donnington Grove, Portswood met as colleagues at the Birmingham and Coventry Cycle Company in Southampton's London Road.

"I didn't like him that much at first. Every time I looked round he was there — I suppose he wore me down in the end," she joked.

They were married at St Edmunds church in The Avenue when Roy got a 48-hour pass from his army base at Fareham.

Roy moved to Pirelli's buying department in Western Esplanade before moving on to Whites Shipyard. He was also a manager for Harland and Wolff.

The couple have three daughters and two sons.

(and 14 grandchildren) 1990

Roy and Clare Hayward celebrated their Diamond Jubilee on September 30 with a thanksgiving mass and will be having a luncheon party at a New Forest Hotel with their family, including 5 children, 16 grandchildren and 5 great grandchildren. They "Named The Day" on September 3, when war was declared and married at St Edmunds Church when Roy was granted 48 hours leave from his army unit.

Clare & Roy in 1999.

My albums have many pictures of this special cousin who is very much like my sister Gladys in her ways and mannerisms.

A very precious couple whose lives I have followed over the years — and have visited four times in England. So have enjoyed meeting their wonderful family.

175

Cousin Clare and I at garden party in our honour in 2000. This was held in Clare and Roy's son Michael's beautiful back garden in Southampton, England. Here you see Michael and Margaret, his friendly wife – an elementary school teacher.

The complete list of Clare and Roy's family in June of 2000 was as follows :

Peter (the oldest) living in Spain and his ex-wife Joy have 4 children-Stephen, married to Carrie-Ann with their child Laura; Mary with children, Tony, Louise, and Becky with child, Jasmine; Michael and his wife Margaret pictured above who have three children – Elizabeth (30), Helen (28) who was living in Australia in 2000 when we were visiting GB, and Charlotte (25) a fun-loving girl who reminded us a little of my grand-daughter, Marnie; Clare & Roy's youngest daughter is Frances, a beautiful, gentle, friendly lady married to a fine Norwegian engineer, Ken Skonnemand, they have three children- Yvette, Karl (married to Faye), and Natalie.

I am enclosing all of these names in case any of you who read this document and in the future make a visit to GB, especially Southampton, you may decide to meet these dear folk.

New President

E. M. WOOLLAMS, B.A., LL.B. is the new president of the Melfort Board of Trade, elected February 6. Mr. Woollams, a graduate of the University of Saskatchewan in 1943, was formerly associated with the law firm of Bastedo and McDougall in Regina, and is now with H. E. Keavin, K.C., in Melfort. He was born at Marriott and spent his boyhood days there.

Back to the story of my life – when in Saskatoon at one of those ballroom dances that I attended with my sailor friend, Angus Mc Tavish, I was delighted to meet again my old schoolmate and neighbour, Eldon Woolliams, who was now making a name for himself as a lawyer, and later to become an MP for Calgary- Bow River. Eldon and his wife, Irva, were enjoying the evening as much as we were.

In late August of 1944 I headed by bus for my new appointment as teacher in Cudworth, Sk. There I joined the staff of Cudworth Public School. I was to teach a Grades 1 & 2 class of 42 children – all RC except one who was the local Doctor's son. My Principal was Eva Kusch (a rare case of a female principal in those days but because so many of the men were away in the war there weren't enough left at home to administer schools). My class was in a separate building.

Not a good picture but it will give you an idea of the numbers in my new class.

PUBLIC & HIGH SCHOOL, CUDWORTH, SASK.

None of the local families wanted to board a teacher so four of us – Nell Stack, Frances Berscheid, and a girl whose parents lived in Humboldt so she went home on week-ends, stayed in the local Cudworth Hotel which was owned and operated by Mrs. Roberge, a vivacious French lady and her family. There didn't appear to be a Mr. Roberge on the scene at any time. Meals were delicious, rooms very small, but we were not far from school which was necessary as none of us had a car, and I hadn't as yet brought my bike up to Cudworth..

Cudworth was a predominantly RC town, with a young dedicated Oblate priest, Father Edward, looking after his flock. On Fridays we teachers accompanied our classes to Mass before school. Our school was a "public" school, not separate or independent so we had our regular visits from the Department of Education "Inspector" as the Superintendent was called in those days.

I recall our first "inspection" – I felt I had everything and everybody in ship-shape form with my 42 little eager beavers all sitting up and squeaky clean. They all politely stood up when Mr. Jones entered and said in unison "Good Morning, Mr. Jones." We had speedily rehearsed this when Miss Kusch had met us teachers before school and warned us of the impending visitation and the customary greeting procedure. But lo! and behold! For the 10 am McLean Printing exercise to practice the letter "p" I had printed on the board loud and clear for the children to copy "P is for pope."

Mr. Jones spotted this first thing as he came in – "Miss Palmer, you must remember, this is a public school, not a Catholic institution. You must not use such subtle ways to influence your students."

So I immediately erased that from the blackboard and substituted " Peter picked a Pumpkin." I hadn't intended to be a missionary even though I did have that hard earned certificate in catechetics.

Otherwise I received a satisfactory report from Mr. Jones, but those four months I spent in Cudworth, other than the fun time I had teaching those lively little primary kids, was the dullest period I ever spent in my whole life. Staying at the hotel, we were never invited to any of the children's homes, our social life was nil except for going to Mass on Sundays and then there was no coffee or socializing after Mass. What a contrast from the friendly Polar Crescent community I had left! How I missed all those dear friends. Frances Berscheid and I went for lots of long walks together in the evenings.

I bought a "Learn How to Crochet" book and with my new craft made many doilies which are still gracing my china cabinets. Then I had the patience to use the finest thread which made the prettiest patterns. When I went home at Christmas I taught my mother how to crochet and she loved it as much as I did. It was indeed my saviour for those long boring evening in a prairie hotel room.

We teachers produced the obligatory Christmas concert which was a resounding success. I had made certain that all 42 of my kids had some part to play in it so all parents would be happy. The good old "Choral Speech" was a wonderful way to absorb them all, and I remember one action song so well – "Little Robin Redbreast." Brings smiles to my heart too. But after the concert we were expected to participate in a boozy party with our Principal and the school board members. I had little experience with the drinks they were mixing – mostly with gin – so I was disgusted and left early.

That evening four of us young teachers decided life was too short to spend as if we were in a monastery – we all resigned. There were a few threats of us losing our teaching certificates because we were breaking our contracts, but we were young and carefree at the time and teachers' jobs were plentiful – the Saskatoon Star Pheonix was full of ads for teachers. The threats were never carried out – perhaps officials asked why not just one, but four teachers were leaving all at once. Perhaps the community would make a greater effort after that to make the teachers feel welcome.

I applied and was accepted to continue the term at Lloydminster Public School teaching forty Grades 2 & 3 students.. My salary was to be $900 per year. I was

179

excited and happy to be going to this interesting town that was situated on the border of Saskatchewan and Alberta with the main street being the dividing line. We would be keeping 2 classroom registers – one for those kids living in SK and one for those in AB. After a loving, wonderful family Christmas holiday at home I was short of money (overspent on Christmas fun) but borrowed $25 from Dad and headed by train for Lloydminster.

Here you see the post card I sent home on my arrival in Lloydminster and the problems I encountered.

Lloydminster area had just opened up as the oil capital of Alberta and Saskatchewan hence the shortage of boarding places. I spent the first week in the hotel but it had no dining room so I had to eat my meals in the local cafes which were full of the oil workers often covered in grease. Besides the added expense of café meals, in those days a woman coming into a café alone was an oddity. I remember the night when an oil well "gushed" as they called it. The cafes were full of men covered in oily coveralls and celebrating - I imagine it went on all night.

Standing with one foot in SK and one in AB I'm now a resident of Lloydminster
but have no home to call my own!

As luck would have it, Mr. Stevenson, the school board secretary, lived right
across the street from the school, and offered me Bed and Breakfast in their
home. That appealed to me, and would cost me much less than the hotel room.
My bedroom was upstairs and I was not allowed to prepare any food in that room
– not even make a sandwich for my lunch at school. Just have cereal and coffee
in their kitchen in the morning, then off to school. Still had to have my evening
meal in a restaurant and pick up a snack in the corner grocery for lunches. While
staying here Mrs. Stevenson taught me how to tat. I found tatting to be the most
difficult craft to learn, but my teacher was fun and very patient. We laughed and
laughed over my attempts but I finally did catch on. As you've probably
gathered I did love to learn.

On Sundays I used to walk home from Mass with a dear little elderly Irish lady,
Mrs. Haynes, who was nearly blind and needed help to make sure she was headed
in the right direction to her home where she lived all by herself. She had lost her
only son in the war. It involved a lot of walking for me back and forth between
her place and the Stevensons. I enjoyed the walking but it did take away from my

marking and lesson preparation time. We became good friends and she invited me in for lunch. Then as we became better acquainted she found out my situation regarding my meals.

"Well, my dear, you are most welcome to come here and have your supper with me – you can prepare whatever you want on my stove, and make yourself a lunch for the next day. I will not charge you a cent. I will be so glad to have your company."

So that worked very well for the whole month of January, then another member of the School board, Reg Wade and his wife Gladys, had previously been caring for Reg's elderly Mother who was living with them. The senior Mrs. Wade had recently passed away so they decided to rent out her bedroom and so provide board and room to another teacher, Lynn Webster who taught Grade 1 and me. We shared the same clothes cupboard, slept in the same bed, and got along just fine – had lots of fun for the next year and a half. Mrs Haynes and I continued having lots of time together – walking to and from church and just keeping in touch with each other.

My new landlady, Mrs. Gladys Wade was a wonderful cook in spite of having terrible rheumatoid arthritis that caused her legs to swell so that she spent a lot of her time in a wheelchair. Her husband, Reg, was out of town a lot – he was working for the Department of Veterans' Affairs helping returned soldiers to get their lives together back at home. Mrs. Wade was glad to have company while Reg was away. They had one adopted teen-aged son, Mervin, a bright, fun-loving kid, who later became a Doctor.

Mrs. Wade taught me how to do petit point needlework. This involved many colours of very fine thread on very fine canvas resulting in very precious pieces of Art. She had one of a dog that had 29 different colours in it. It was amazingly beautiful. She created many of these fine works of art as she sat in her wheelchair. She also collected Spode fine china which she used every day. I always dried the dishes and was terrified I might drop a piece but never did. Reg would bring her home a surprise piece of Spode each time he returned from a business trip. They were such a dear loving couple and so good to me.

Above is a photo of the first piece of petit point I created. I framed it and gave it to Mother and Dad for the Christmas of 1945. It was hanging in our home on the farm, later in their homes in Kelowna, and Victoria. When Mother took up residence in Oak Bay Lodge she gave it back to me and now it hangs in our master bedroom.

Mrs. Wade and I used to have lots of long talks and she gave me many good words of advice. I told her of my plans to go further afield in my teaching. By this time I was really thinking about choosing BC as my home for a couple of years because I had a yen to travel. But as I mentioned before I was not doing very well at saving my money.

Mrs. Wade said " The only way to reach your goal is to find out how much money you'll need, how long you have to save that money, and then decide how much you have to put away each month to reach that amount, make up your mind that you will never tap into that nest egg, and you'll do what you want to do."

When I had told my parents of my dream, Dad (from whom I'd just borrowed the $25) said "Oh, Agnes, that's the biggest joke I've heard in a long time! You'll never save up enough money to do that."

It must have been a combination of Mrs.Wade's advice and Dad's roundabout challenge added to my stubborn determination that made me decide I would go out to BC at the end of June in 1946. I set my sights on doing just that.

My Lloydminster friends and fellow teachers - front row from left to right – me, Joyce Burge, Mildred Larsen. Back row – Lynn Webster on the right and I can't recall the name of the other girl. Joyce Burge and I became very close friends.

In the Christmas holidays of 1945 Lynn married Jim Bryans who owned and operated the local Mens' Wear store so after that I had the whole bedroom to myself. I thought I was in heaven!! My plans for going to BC were still dancing around in my head, and I had in my savings account 4 x $35 = $140 toward my dream.

Among my first letters I received in Lloydminster was one from Donald McNab saying that he had met someone special and was going to be married – so our engagement was over. I immediately mailed back to him his ring and all his photos and keepsakes and wished him well. So much for that long distance friendship. I wasn't going to spend all my energy in mourning for that dead relationship – Mother's words of warning about falling in love with a service man had proven to be true.

I signed up for an evening typing course at the local high school taught by Hazel Miller, who became a very good friend. She was a victim of that dreaded disease, polio, and had to get around with crutches, but had such a wonderful happy disposition, a good teacher, and drove around in her specially designed car which was usually full of us girls- all in our 20's.

There were dances every Saturday night in the Lloydminster Hall – as I've mentioned before, we girls had to dance with each other a lot of the time – the men who were left at home in wartime were rejects from the military, but very popular at the dances. I remember going to dances with Henry Dougan, who also had a nurse girl friend whom he later married (those nurses were our greatest opponents for the available dates!) and he had a friend whose name I can't recall who was also of poor health but was a very good dancer.

A card I created for Mother around this time. I continued occupying my spare time with my hobbies - watercolour painting, crocheting, tatting and petit point.

Joy of joys! On May 8, 1945, Germany surrendered to the Allies, and the war in Europe was over so now after six long years of a terrible war we would have peace in our country once again. What a cause for celebration! Our boys and girls would be coming home!

I'll never forget V-E Day in Lloydminster. Five of us girls piled into Hazel's car, singing and shouting twenty-five miles to Kitscoty, AB to a victory dance. Hazel couldn't dance but she was such fun to be with, and enjoyed watching the rest of us having a good time.

But there was still war going on in the Pacific region of the world, and some of our boys and girls, after VE day, volunteered to serve in that area. Gary and Francis' father, Johnny Graf, did just that so he was sent home right away for a leave before being shipped over to the Orient. But joy of joys! The Japanese surrendered on August 14, 1945 so that meant that Johnny, and all the soldiers, sailors and airmen and women could stay home for all time. What a thankful feeling of relief and peace! I did not get to meet Johnny Graf until November of 1946.

When I went home for the summer holidays of 1945 Bob Pearce (who had been overseas for 4 years) arrived home with the end of the war. Wow! How he had changed, from the pimply kid I used to play darebase and softball with when we visited the Pearce family near Harris, into this mature good-looking gentleman. Perhaps you remember- his brother was my SNS Grad date. We always had close ties with this family. I really think Mrs. Pearce was hoping one of her boys would talk me into being her daughter-in-law. She was one of my special friends and we corresponded for years, exchanging crochet, knitting, and embroidery patterns. A very dear lady!

Bob must have also noticed that while he was overseas I too had matured and soon asked me to go out with him to the various dances and picnics of that summer. He was a fine person and we enjoyed the times we spent together. He knew that I was planning to head for BC within the next year.

In these rare photos you see Bob Pearce in an army tent and trench in Germany. He would never have been allowed to send this in his letters which were censored, but he did manage to bring these two snapshots home when he returned after the war ended in 1945.

Back to Lloydminster I went with my plan to put $35 of my monthly cheque from my $90 (I was now getting $900 per year) into savings for that dreamed of trip to BC.

In my mail one day in the next March, (1946) there arrived a letter from Angus McTavish along with a beautiful "To my Sweetheart" valentine, and the joyful news that he was out of hospital, perfectly cured of TB, with an honourable discharge and generous lifelong pension from the Navy. He had bought a car and was planning to come and visit me in Lloydminster. His sister lived in a neighbouring town of Marshall, SK . There she and her husband, Maurice Palmer (not a relative) ran an experimental farm. Angus said, in his letter, that we could spend the week-end with them.

So in June, Angus arrived in Lloydminster for a week. He stayed at the local hotel, took me out to dinner each evening, met Mrs. Haynes (who just loved him), the Wades, and all my girl friends. On Friday after school we headed out to Marshall to his sister's place – they were beautiful people who welcomed us into their lovely home. My bedroom had a wonderful view out into their vegetable and flower garden which was surrounded by lush evergreen trees. Being a government owned farm they had the very best of irrigation and treatment.

Angus and I talked a lot about the future and my plans to go to BC for a couple of years. He was happy for me - especially for my planned six weeks to be spent in Victoria. He was very fond of that city, having been in the Navy stationed in Esquimalt. He said Victoria was his favourite city of all the cities he had seen in his recent world travels. He told me to be sure to see Butchart Gardens and the Crystal Pool and ballroom.

Angus had his own plans of settling on the home farm in Asquith as his younger brother was doing. His father owned a big dairy and wheat farm just west of Polar Crescent School. Angus wanted me to promise I would go out to that farm for a visit after summer school was over in Victoria, before I went to my teaching position. I made no promises for two reasons- I knew I would be flat broke by that time so wouldn't be able to afford the trip, and I also knew my Dad would not approve of my going to stay in a boy friend's home with no other women there. Angus's mother had died a few years before. His father and brother Gordon lived there with him. Angus and I said good-bye with promises to write often.

My plans continued as I finished out my school term at Lloydminster. I thought to myself. " If I'm going to 'the coast' as the prairie people still call BC, and since I plan to teach out there for a couple of years, I will be required to get some credits from a BC University to make my SK certificate valid for BC." Immediately I registered and paid the required tuition to the Victoria Summer School. By the end of June I had $350 in my savings, and a promise of a teaching job for $1000 per annum in a 16 room Elementary Jr. Sr. High school at Rutland, BC. Principal was D. H. Campbell.

With that and my end of June salary I had enough to buy my a flat steamer trunk to hold all my worldly goods (including my treasured set of World Book now finally completely paid for), a one-way CN train ticket (complete with berth), and a bunk bed reserved in an Evangel Tabernacle Church dorm at 448 North Park Street, Victoria, BC with 36 other girls from all over the world.

My good friend, Irene Dougan, went as far as Edmonton with me on the CN train. We stayed overnight there. Irene's sister lived in Victoria and I planned to look her up.

It was June 30, 1946 and I was headed for BC!